THE BOOK THE SCRIBE

THE BOOK THE SCRIBE

VOLUME I

JULIE MARTIN

INTRODUCTION

THIS BOOK IS A COMPILATION OF WRITINGS GIVEN TO "THE SCRIBE" FROM THE SOULS OF PEOPLE IN HEAVEN AND THE SOULS OF PEOPLE LIVING ON EARTH. MANY ARE HIGH PROFILE PEOPLE FROM HISTORY AND CELEBRITIES FROM THE PAST AND LIVING (A FEW WRITINGS ARE FROM HIGH PROFILE PEOPLE THAT ARE IN THE LOWER REALMS). ALL WRITINGS ARE GIVEN IN A POETIC STYLE. THE FOCUS OF THE WRITINGS BRINGS THE READER TO THINK ABOUT THEIR LIFE PURPOSE AND HOW THERE IS A NEW, HIGHER INTER-DIMENSIONAL WAY OF LIVING, INVOLVING ANGELS, THE HOLY SPIRIT OF GOD AND A PERSON'S HIGHER SELF. HEALING THE WORLD IS EMPHASIZED. GIVING AND TAKING CARE OF ALL THOSE WHO HAVE LESS OR HAVE NEEDS IS POUNDED HOME IN THESE WRITINGS. PAST SINS OF HIGH PROFILE PEOPLE ARE BROUGHT TO LIGHT AND A NEW WAY OF THINKING AND LIVING IS EXPOUNDED ON. THE NAME JESUS IS PREVALENT THROUGHOUT AND PROFOUND WRITINGS FROM JESUS, SAINTS, ANGELS, WORLD LEADERS, AND RELIGIOUS LEADERS FROM ALL RELIGIONS, BRING THE REALITY OF THE OTHER WORLDS TO THIS EARTH - SO THAT READERS CAN HEAR WHAT THEY HAVE TO SAY.

PREFACE

My Name Is Julie
Thoughts Are Rare
I Live In Spirit Atmosphere
An Accident I Had Or Two
It Gave Me Special Spirit View
So Write "The Book" I Did Was Called
To Break Through Holy Spirit Walls

The Scribe

Note To Readers: The Writings From The Scribe Are
Perfectly Imperfect.

CONTENTS

INTRODUCTION · V
PREFACE · VII

SEGMENT I

PRINCESS DIANA – QUEEN OF HEARTS · · · · · · · · · · · 3
DRUGS · 4
WRITERS · 5
THE VATICAN · 6
SUZE ORMAN · 8
MEXICANS · 9
ATHEIST · 10
CONVENTS · 11
RUDE AWAKENING!! · 12
BRUCE LEE · 13
WINSTON CHURCHILL "THE BLITZ" · · · · · · · · · · · · · · 14
FRIGHTENED (SARAH) · 16
BEA BRIGHT · 18
LEPERS · 20
ALEXANDER THE GREAT!!?? · · · · · · · · · · · · · · · · · · · 22
JEWS · 24
JOHN · 25
DOMINIC SPIRIT IN HELL!! · 26

STEVEN SURFER DUDE SPIRIT · 28
CIVIL WAR MAN · 30
ABRAHAM LINCOLN – SOLDIERS · · · · · · · · · · · · · · · · 32
ABRAHAM LINCOLN · 33
SHARON-SPIRIT · 34
ELVIS PRESLEY · 36
ANGELS, SAINTS, JESUS, SAINT JOSEPH · · · · · · · · · · · · · · 37
GUARDIAN ANGELS!! · 38
JANIS JOPLIN · 39
SARAH-IN HEAVEN · 40
BOB DYLAN ·41
KURT COBAIN · 42
JESUS · 43
GEISHA-ARTIST · 44
THE LOUVRE · 45
CAT STEVENS · 46
SIR LAURENCE OLIVIER · 47
JOHN DENVER · 48
JACK THE RIPPER · 50
FRENCH PROSTITUTES · 52
JESUS KNOWS ALL!! SEES ALL!! KNOW THAT!! · · · · · · · · · 54
MARRIAGE · 55
GAYS JESUS · 56
GAYS AND ANGELS · 57
ELVIS PRESLEY · 58
HELEN KELLER · 59
DOMINIC VISIT FROM HELL!! · · · · · · · · · · · · · · · · · · · 60
KING HENRY THE EIGHTH ·61
JACQUELINE KENNEDY ONASSIS · · · · · · · · · · · · · · · · · 62
ANNE FRANK · 63
ADOLF HITLER · 64
ADOLF HITLER · 65
CELINE DION · 66

SAINT QUEEN ELIZABETH THE 1ST · · · · · · · · · · · · · · · · · · 67
MARRIAGE · 68
FATHER FRANCIS · 69
STEVEN SPIRIT · 70
DALAI LAMA · 72
PATRICK SWAYZE · 73
ROBERT PATTINSON · 74
BRAD PITT · 76
AMISH ANGELS · 77
JULIA CHILD · 78
BRUCE LEE · 80
BLIND ANGELS · 82
BRITTANY MURPHY · 84
CORY HAIM · 86
BILL GATES · 87
WARREN BUFFETT · 88
PRINCESS DIANA · 90
THOMAS JEFFERSON · 92
JOHNNY CASH · 94
JIMI HENDRIX · 95
JOHN LENNON · 96
SALLY HEMINGS (SLAVE) · 98
MARILYN MONROE · 100
ABRAHAM LINCOLN - SLAVES · · · · · · · · · · · · · · · · · · · 101
GEORGE WASHINGTON ·102
THEODORE ROOSEVELT ·103
HANK WILLIAMS ·104
COLIN FIRTH ·105
PATSY CLINE ·106
THE KENNEDY FAMILY ·108
MARTHA WASHINGTON · 110
MARIE ANTOINETTE · 112
PRINCE CHARLES · 113

LADY GAGA · 114
MARY TODD LINCOLN · 116
THE CIVIL WAR WOMEN · 118
ELEANOR ROOSEVELT · 120
WOMEN OF "THE DEPRESSION" · 122
JEFFREY DAHMER · 124
SARAH (GHOST)!!!! · 126
JOHN WAYNE · 128
JIMI HENDRIX · 129
STEPHEN KING · 130
JESUS · 131
FRANCES BEAN COBAIN · 132
JACKIE GLEASON · 134
SPECIAL ANGELS · 135
HEATH LEDGER · 136
FRANK LLOYD WRIGHT (GENIUS) · · · · · · · · · · · · · · · · · · 138
"THE GREAT QUEEN VICTORIA" · · · · · · · · · · · · · · · · · · · 140
ANDREW CARNEGIE · 142
TOM CRUISE · 144
DOUBT · 145
BENJAMIN FRANKLIN · 146
JACK · 148
ASIAN MAN · 150
ROSA PARKS · 152
MOTHER TERESA · 154
WILLIAM JEFFERSON CLINTON · 155
ANNE FRANK · 156
JOHN AND JACKIE · 158
HELEN KELLER · 160
ELEANOR ROOSEVELT · 161
THOMAS EDISON · 162
ABRAHAM LINCOLN · 164
JACKIE CHAN · 165

WILLIAM SHAKESPEARE ·166
WILLIAM SHAKESPEARE "KNIGHT" · · · · · · · · · · · · · · · ·168
GENERAL WILLIAM SHERMAN · · · · · · · · · · · · · · · ·170
SIR EDMUND HILLARY · 171
KATHARINE HEPBURN ·172
JOHN WAYNE ·174
RUSSELL CROWE ·176
PERSIAN WOMEN!! ·178
WOMEN OF THE HOLOCAUST · · · · · · · · · · · · · · · ·180
ALBERT EINSTEIN ·182
VINCENT VAN GOGH ·183
SEPHARDIC ANGEL ·184
CHRISTOPHER COLUMBUS · · · · · · · · · · · · · · · · · ·186
CAESAR AUGUSTUS ·188
THE HOLY PROPHET MUHAMMAD · · · · · · · · · · · · ·190
HARRIET BEECHER STOWE · · · · · · · · · · · · · · · · ·192
WOLFGANG AMADEUS MOZART · · · · · · · · · · · · · · ·194
MICHAEL JACKSON ·196
LUDWIG VAN BEETHOVEN · · · · · · · · · · · · · · · · · ·198
PABLO PICASSO · 200
J.R.R. TOLKIEN · 202
JUDY GARLAND · 203
STEPHEN HAWKING · 204
MOTORCYCLES · 206
CHILDREN OF THE HOLOCAUST · · · · · · · · · · · · · · 207
JOHN FITZGERALD KENNEDY · · · · · · · · · · · · · · · 208
KING JOSEPH STALIN · 209

SEGMENT II

GILDA RADNER · 213
BOB DYLAN · 214
JOHN DENVER · 215
CHARLTON HESTON · 216

DEANNA DURBIN · 217
CHRISTOPHER REEVE ·218
JOHN LENNON ·219
JANIS JOPLIN · 220
THE HOLY PROPHET MUHAMMAD · · · · · · · · · · · · · · · ·221
ANGELS OF THE AIR · 222
STEPHEN SONDHEIM · 223
SONNY BONO · 224
ANNELIES MARIE FRANK · 225
JOHN THE BAPTIST · 226
SAINT PATRICK · 227
FATIMA · 228
SAINT RITA HAYWORTH · 229
SAINT AUDREY HEPBURN · 230
SAINT AUDREY HEPBURN ·231
MERYL STREEP · 232
SIR WINSTON CHURCHILL · 234
SIR THOMAS KINKADE · 235
ELIZABETH · 236
PATRICK SWAYZE · 237
ROBIN WILLIAMS · 238
JOHN LENNON · 239
ANGELS - THE SURETIES · 240
JOHN BELUSHI ·241
STEPHEN KING · 242
STEVEN TYLER · 243
MARGARET THATCHER · 244
ANGELS - THE ANSWERS · 245
KING HENRY THE VIII · 246
MARGARET THATCHER · 248
STEPHEN KING · 249
DOCTOR OZ · 250
SAINT JOAN OF ARC ·251

SAINT STEPHEN ·252
SAINT STEPHEN, THE MARTYR · · · · · · · · · · · · · · · · · · · 253
NAPOLEON BONAPARTE ·254
SIR WINSTON CHURCHILL · 255
KHADIJA PROPHET OF GOD ·256
IMAM ALI · 257
HAGAR MOTHER OF ISLAM ·258
FATIMA ·259
MUHAMMAD PROPHET OF GOD · · · · · · · · · · · · · · · · · ·260
BERNIE SANDERS ·261
PRINCE ·262
HARRIET BEECHER STOWE ·263
THOMAS KINKADE · 264
THE QUIET MAN ·265
THE QUIET MAN ·266
THE QUIET MAN ·267
FATIMA ·268
MOTHER'S TEARS ·269
THE HOLY PROPHET MUHAMMAD · · · · · · · · · · · · · · ·270
FATHER ABRAHAM · 271
THOMAS KINKADE ·272
KING GEORGE VI ·273
THOMAS EDISON ·274
NIKOLA TESLA ·275
NORDIC ANGELS ·276
NORDIC ANGELS ·277
NORDIC ANGELS ·278
NORDIC ANGELS ·279
KING LOUIS XIV OF FRANCE · · · · · · · · · · · · · · · · · · ·280
IRISH MARTYRS · 281
PRESIDENT RONALD REAGAN · · · · · · · · · · · · · · · · · · 282
SIR ISAAC NEWTON ·284
ABRAHAM LINCOLN · 285

PRESIDENT GERALD FORD · 286
ARCTIC ANGELS · 287
ARCTIC ANGELS · 288
ARCTIC ANGELS · 289
ABRAHAM LINCOLN · 290
PRESIDENT GEORGE WASHINGTON · · · · · · · · · · · · · · · · ·291
ARCTIC ANGELS · 292
ROCKY MOUNTAIN ANGELS · · · · · · · · · · · · · · · · · · · 293
HIMALAYAN ANGELS · 294
NORDIC ANGELS · 295
PRESIDENT BARACK OBAMA · · · · · · · · · · · · · · · · · · · 296
IMAM HUSAYN – ISLAM · 297

INDEX · 299

Segment I

Princess Diana – Queen Of Hearts

Note: 7:30pm

I Need To Know You're Here, You Know
To Let The "Holy Spirit" Show
A Drab Dark Past The Church Has Been
Just Greed And Lies A Wicked Den
But Time Has Come You Know It's True
To Rattle Cages, Evil Flu
Cause Sick Has Been And Prison "See"
The Trappings Of The Christian Tree
So Chop It Down You Know We Can
And Build A House To Heal The "Man"
Cause Man Has Caused Much Harm On Earth!!
It's Time To Rule The Women's Worth!!
My Darling Dear You're Chosen Be
To Rock The World With Healing Breeze
You'll Release Wind To Cleanse The Land
A Bright New Day You Understand
So Give Us Paper, Give Us Pen
Will Write Your Book New York Top Ten!!

Love,
Diana
Your Friend

DRUGS

NOTE: WRITTEN 9:20PM

THE LEPER SOUL IS COMMONPLACE
IS FILLED WITH WEB'S DECEPTIVE LACE
THE PILLS YOU TAKE THEY CANNOT FORM
A NEW SOUL SKIN A CROWN ADORNED
WITH HEAVEN'S LIGHTS AND HEAVEN'S LOVE
JUST HAVE TO GET IT FROM ABOVE
IT IS FREE FOR EVERYONE FROM HERE
JUST HAVE TO BREAK FROM SIN AND FEAR
THE WAY TO DO IT CLEAN AND RIGHT
JUST OFFER UP YOUR SOUL TONIGHT
TO JESUS CHRIST THE SON OF GOD
THE MASTER KEY THE UNLOCK GOD
HE'LL SET YOU FREE FROM PAIN AND FRIGHT
AND BRING YOU INTO JOYFUL LIGHT!!

WRITERS

NOTE: THIS WRITING WAS GIVEN TO ME AFTER I HAD SEEN "THE OTHER BOLEYN GIRL". ALSO HAD GONE TO "ROMAN" EXHIBIT AT AN ART MUSEUM. WAS VERY SPIRITUAL THAT DAY.

FREEDOMS COME AND FREEDOMS GO
DESTINY A WHIFF OF SNOW
CAUSE EVERY DAY'S A MEMORY SOON
WE HAVE TO MAKE THE ROOM TO BLOOM!!
A WRITER HAS A BLOCK TO THINK
HE HAS CONTROL OF PEN AND INK
BUT WHAT HE THINKS HE DOES NOT KNOW
THAT GOD IS IN THE CHARGE OF SHOW!!
CAUSE EVERY LETTER WORD IS PLANNED
IT DOESN'T TAKE MUCH UNDERSTAND
ALL MESSAGES ARE FROM ABOVE
BELOW BENEATH COME FROM THE DOVE
THE HOLY SPIRIT SOME WILL SAY
WOULD ONLY WRITE THE WORDS SO GAY!!
BUT TRULY SONS AND DAUGHTERS HEAR
THE HOLY SPIRIT CAN WRITE FEAR!!
CAUSE GOD'S IN CHARGE YOU UNDERSTAND
OF EVERY BOOK THAT HIT THE LAND!!
YOU SOMETIMES THINK A BOOK IS JUNK
BUT MYSTERIES UNRAVEL STUMP!!
THE LORD, YES JESUS CHRIST YOU SEE
COULD PICK UP ANY BOOK THAT HE
WOULD WANT TO TRANSLATE WHAT IT'S WORTH
AND SPILL THE BEANS WHY GAVE IT BIRTH!!

The Vatican

NOTE: 9:24AM
I WENT TO SEE THE DA VINCI CODE LAST NIGHT. WOKE
UP IN THE MORNING. HAD SAINT FAUSTINA, JESUS, SAINT
TERESA OF AVILA AND SAINT THERESA OF LISIEUX STANDING
AT THE FOOT OF MY BED.
    THIS IS WHAT THEY SAID.

TROUBLED MINDS AND TROUBLED HEARTS
CAN'T TAKE THE CHURCH THE FILTH THE ROT
THE VATICAN THEY LAY A CLAIM
THEY OWN THE RIGHTS ON JESUS' NAME
THE VISION'S CLEAR GOD WANTS SOULS FREE
NOT BOWING DOWN ON BENDED KNEE
TO MEN IN RED AND PURPLE ROBES
LET'S FEED THE POOR THE SICK THE OLD
THE CHURCH'S WEALTH MUST NEVER BE
TO SPEND ON YACHTS AND LUXURY!!
THE DIMES AND DOLLARS GIVEN THERE
MUST SPEND ON HALLS THAT NEED REPAIR
AND TAKE CARE THINGS, YES MAKE THEM NICE
BUT, NO PRIEST SHOULD BE THROWING DICE
WITH TRIPS ABROAD TO LAY IN SUN
TO PICK UP BOYS OR GIRLS FOR FUN
NO GOD'S DELIGHT IS NOT IN THAT
HE WANTS TO SEE THE POOR FED FAST!!!
THE PAINS THE SCREAMS ARE HELD IN ARMS
OF LOVE YOU SEE THIS KNITTED YARD
OF WOOL IT MUST BRING BLANKETS WARM
TO ALL GOD'S CHILDREN DARK AND BLONDE

He Loves The Ones In North And South
And East And West Go Search Them Out
The Tattered Rags The Calloused Feet
Are Royal Robes And Prince's Shoes
The Ones We See And Look Away
Cause Poverty Ain't Pretty Play
It Makes Us Feel So Sad To See
The Channels Turned On Your T.V.
Must Write A Check, Yes Send Some Cash
To Set Them Free The Royal Cast!!

Amen

Suze Orman

Note: Took Writing 3:59am
Had been reading book by Suze Orman "Women and Money". Woke up, saw Suze standing illuminated next to my bed. This was the first writing she gave me.

Just Look Inside Your Soul And See
A Money Tree That's Filled With Glee!!!
For Poverty Is Life Of PAIN!!!!
Of WORRIES!!! STRESS!!! And Lots Of STRAIN!!!
I've Come From Heaven Come To Earth
To Bring A Ticket To Your Purse!!!
A Golden Ticket!! Golden Pass!!
To Money Worries In The Past!!!!
I'll Take you To A Land Where Free
And Peace Of Mind Is Where You'll Be!!!!
I See The Chains The Prison Cells
Are Filled With "Dames" Stiletto Heels!!!
Cause Wealthy Deep Inside Not Feel!!!
So Nordstrom Rack Before The Bills!!!
Cause When I'm Dressing Fancy Free
A Momentary Kind Of Glee!!!
It Feels My Soul It Feels My Thoughts
Till Finance Worry Stresses Rot!!!
The Fancy Free I'd Like To Feel
Is Covered Overwhelmed With "Bills"!!!!!

Suze

Mexicans

Had souls of immigrant farm workers standing around me. They gave me this writing.

Your Neighbours Down South, Don't You See Us At All??
American Wealth, Yes You Stand White And Tall!!
You Cross To Our Border, Get Drunk And Have Sex!!
Ignore We Cry Calling, "Please Help Us Get Fed!!"
You Spend All Your Money, Seems You Throw It Away
On Alcohol Nights, Where You Dance Oh So Gay!!
We Cross At Your Borders, Oh Dark In The Night
We're Scared With Our Families, And Shaking With Fright!!
We Come Do Your Work, On Our Hands And Our Knees
Get Paid Nothing Wages, Oh White Man Is Pleased!!!
We Work On Your Farms, Pick The Fruit Off Your Trees
And Live In Disgrace, In This Land Filled With Greed!!
You're Stupid And Blind, To Our Plight To Our Needs
You Take Us To Jail, And In Buses Police Beat Us Black And To Blue!!
So Listen My Story, Cause Yes It Is True
Your Wonderful Nation, The Red White And Blue!!!

Atheist

My Atheist Oh I Love And Adore
They Give Up Their Faith
So The World Can Have More!!

Atheist Are So Holy!!

Give Up Spiritual Comfort For Others!!

Jesus

Convents

The Kind Of Prayers They Said In Past
Was Dynamite Created Blast!!
For All The Souls The World To See
They Broke Through Gates From You To Me!!

Jesus

Rude Awakening!!

Yes Those That Hold On Money Tight
Are Doomed To Torture Terror Fright!!
I Have No Mercy Understand
To Souls Who Live With Greedy Hands!!
Inherit Curse They Will From Me
To Break It Oh It's Hard You See!!
Eternity Has Got A Claus
A Trust Adhere To Generous Laws!!
But If You Break Them Dare Not Give
You'll Wish This Life You've Never Lived!!

Jesus

Bruce Lee

Note: 7:07pm
At Bruce Lee's grave. He is here.

Children, Children, Understand
Power Give You In Your Hands!!
Want To Make You Know What's Right
Power Surges In You Knight!!
Don't You Know That When You Pray
Shackles Melt And Fade Away!!
For My Darling I Will Cry
When I Teach You How To Fly!!
Heights Will Reach That Carry Truths
Healing Touches Show You Proof!!

So High You Will Go, So Happy, So Blessed

Love, Bruce

WINSTON CHURCHILL "THE BLITZ"

NOTE: 3:28PM
WINSTON CHURCHILL WAS STANDING IN FRONT OF ME, BY MY DESK. I WAS VERY EXCITED TO SEE HIS SOUL. DON'T THINK I'VE SEEN HIM BEFORE. MY MOTHER HAD BEEN TALKING TO ME ABOUT "THE BLITZ". FELT THAT I WAS GOING TO RECEIVE A WRITING, AND I WAS RIGHT. WINSTON BROUGHT IT TO ME.

BOMBS ARE BLASTING EVERYWHERE
YOU TRY TO HIDE BUT SAFE NOT HERE!!
A LITTLE SECRET PLACE YOU KNOW
IT HAS A SHELTER BOMBS CAN'T BLOW!!
THE NUNS THE PRIESTS THEY PRAY TO FIGHT
TO BRING THE ANGELS IN "THE LIGHT"!!
CAUSE DARKNESS FILLS THE NIGHT WITH FEAR
AND DAYS ARE DAMP AND GLOOMY WHERE
THE DEVILS LURK THEY FILL THE SKIES
IN FIGHTER PLANES THEY LAUGH WE CRY!!
I SHAKE I SHOOK I THOUGHT WAS NEAR
THE END OF WORLD THE TIME WAS HERE!!
BUT IN THE END IT TURNED OUT RIGHT
OUR SPIRIT CHANGED THE DARKNESS BRIGHT!!
OUR BRITISH PEOPLE LIVED TO TELL

Amazing Stories Country Dwell!!
They Shared Their Food And Shared The Land
It Brought Them Close A Spirit Grand!!

The War!!
Suffering Spiritual Fertilizer!!

Love To You All!!

Winston

Frightened (Sarah)

NOTE: 4:27PM
I AM SITTING AT MY DESK READING A BOOK. A GIRL IS STANDING IN FRONT OF ME. SHE LOOKS AROUND 20 YEARS OLD WITH SHOULDER LENGTH BROWN HAIR. HER FACE LOOKS PRETTY, THEN KEEPS CHANGING, LOOKING GHOULISH, SCARY.

SHE SAID HER NAME WAS SARAH. SHE HAD HEARD MY PRAYERS AND FELT THAT I COULD POSSIBLY PRAY HER HOME.

AS SHE WAS GIVING ME THIS WRITING ANGELS CAME INTO THE ROOM (SAW THEM OPEN UP THE CEILING, VERY BRIGHT LIGHT) AND SHE WAS LEVITATING BACKWARDS INTO THE LIGHT THANKING ME FOR PRAYING.

SHE RETURNED A FEW MONTHS LATER AND GAVE ME ANOTHER WRITING ABOUT THE REASON SHE HAD BEEN STUCK AND UNDER A CURSE.

I AM A SPIRIT A GHOST YOU KNOW
I'M LOCKED IN RAGE AND CAN'T LET GO!!
I NEED SOMEBODY PRAY FOR ME
JUST PLEASE FORGIVE AND SET ME FREE!!
I WANDER WALKING STREETS OF MAN
I ENTER IN AT NIGHTS I STAND
BESIDE YOUR BED JUST LOOKING IN
I SUCK YOUR SOUL THAT I MAY LIVE
CAUSE BREATH OF LIFE I TAKE FROM YOU
I SEND YOU INTO NIGHTMARE VIEW!!
YOUR SOUL WILL SEE WHERE I COME FROM
THIS LOWER PLACE THE DEVILS RUN
ETERNITY IT SEEMS SO LONG
BUT PRAY FOR ME I WILL BE STRONG!!

I Hear Your Prayers The Songs You Sing
They Take Away The Hells Bells Ring!!
So Glad I Am That I've Found You
You'll Punch A Hole And Get Me Through!!
Oh Now I See It Heavens Clear
The Angels Come And Draw Me Near!!

Thank You!!! Thank You!!! Thank You!!!

Praise The Lord!!! Thank You!!!

(She said as she was being received into Heaven)

Bea Bright

NOTE: WRITTEN 9:20AM
WRITING STARTED COMING IN AS I WAS BRUSHING MY TEETH.
  BEA, AN ELDERLY WOMAN I HAD KNOWN, STARTED APPEARING TO ME AT WORK. THEN APPEARED IN MY HOUSE AND GAVE ME THIS WRITING. SHE WAS BORN 1912 AND DIED IN MID-2000.

I HAD A LENS A TYPE OF VIEW
OF DAYS GONE PAST WHEN CARS WERE NEW
WE HAD SOME BUGGY'S AND HORSES FEW
AS LITTLE GIRL I RODE THEM TOO!!
MY LIFE WAS HARD WHEN WAR BEGAN
MY MOTHER, FATHER WAS FRIGHTENED THEN
THE SOLDIERS MARCHED WE SAW ON REELS
WHEN WORLD WAR ONE WAS AT THEIR HEELS!!
I WANT TO TELL YOU PLEASE HEAR MY PLIGHT
PLEASE LISTEN DEAR, PLEASE LISTEN WRITE/RIGHT!!
CAUSE WE HOLD SPECIAL BLESSINGS, KNOW
THE SOULS THAT LIVED LONG TIME AGO!!
I WANT YOU TEACH THIS WORLD OF OURS
SOME SPECIAL KNOWLEDGE NEW KIND OF LAWS!!
CAUSE SOMEHOW BLIND THE WORLD HAS BEEN
AND NOT SO KIND A DEVIL'S DEN
I WANT TO TELL YOU TO MAKE YOU KNOW
I HAVE A SPECIAL VIEW TO SHOW!!
YOU'LL SEE THINGS CLEARLY WITH MY OLD EYES
THEY CARRY GIFTS A KIND SURPRISE!!
JUST KNOCK, KNOCK, KNOCK, YES KNOCK ON WOOD

I'll Open Doors To Bring You Food!!
You'll Feed The Earth A Fresh New Stew
That Carries In It Blessings Glue!!
To Bond Us Right A Brand New Man
Who Walks In All Religions Brand!!
No More Divisions Can You See Dear,
The Walls Are Not Allowed Not Here!!
Cause This New Place We're Living In
Is Heaven Space, A New Begin!!
This Global Plan I've Seen It Through
The Eyes Of God It's Beauty's True!!
So Don't You Fret And Don't You Fear
Cause Dark Cold Days Their End Is Hear/Here!!
The Lord's Excited, Reveal His Plan
To Bring To Happiness (Happy) Every Man!!
Cause Deep Inside We Have A Spring
To Tap It's Flow, The World Must Sing!!
A New Relationship To God
Is Waiting For The Pipes Unclog!!
We Have To Flush Them Tune Them Up
To Bring The World To Holy Sup!!
You See, You'll Feast On Love That's Bright
My Name Is Bea And This I Write!!

(Thank you!! Julie is a Ghostwriter!! For real!!)

Ha !! Ha!! Ha!!

Bea

LEPERS

NOTE: JUST WOKE UP. 3:58AM
HAD WATCHED NATIONAL GEOGRAPHIC SPECIAL ON LEPERS
THIS NIGHT BEFORE GOING TO BED. THE ANGELIC SOULS OF
THE LEPERS CAME TO ME IN THE NIGHT AND GAVE ME THIS
WRITING.

WE ARE LEPERS DON'T YOU KNOW
THE EXILES OF THE WORLD WE GO
INTO SOME HOMES INTO SOME LANDS
IN COLONIES YOU UNDERSTAND!!
WE ARE NOT SINNERS NO NOT OUR LOT
WE ARE A MARTYR TYPE THAT ROTS!!
YOU LOOK AT US AND GRUESOME GROW
A ROOT OF HATE AND JUDGEMENT KNOW
WE CANNOT BLAME THE LOOK IN EYES
WE KNOW DISGUST IS OUR SURPRISE!!
WE FRIGHTEN SCARE OUR FELLOW MAN
IT'S WORSE THAN AIDS YOU UNDERSTAND!!
OUR LIMBS THEY MELT OUR EYES GO BLIND
A SICKNESS OF A DIFFERENT KIND!!
THE HISTORY OF PAIN WILL SHOW
THE DOCUMENTED SHAME WE KNOW!!
THE PAIN THAT HURTS OUR HEART THE MOST
IS EXILE FROM OUR FAMILY TOAST!!
WE MISS OUR LOVE FROM FAMILY TREE
WHEN WE WERE HUGGED AND KISSED FOR FREE!!
SO LISTEN TO US LISTEN CLOSE
WE'RE POWERFUL OF HEAVENS MOST!!

ONE LOOK INTO OUR EYES YOU'LL SEE
A HEALING GIFT THAT COMES FROM ME!!
"THE MARTYRS OF LEPROSY!!"

SUPER POWERS, DYNAMITE POWER,
HEALERS, ANGELS!!!

Alexander The Great!!??

Note: Just woke up. 1:03am
Alexander was at the foot of my bed in shackles.
Had men surrounding him, guards. Begging me to
get up and take this writing. It was very hard to
wake up, so tired, exhausted.

Oh You See This Mask I Wear
Is Filled With Courage Fighting Fear!!
But Have To Say I Conquered Land
With Criminal An Ego Stand!!
You Mustn't Know You Mustn't Think
How Brave I Was Know That I Stink!!
I Killed Some Children Burned Some Men
Raped Some Women Ate Some Hens!!
This Greed This Power That I Wear
Is Filled With Sin, Yes Everywhere!!
I Want You Darling Say A Prayer
I Need Them Much I Suffer Rare!!
Cause Everything I Said And Did
I Pay The Consequence I Live!!
I Suffer Rape And Torment Much
I Live In Hell The Devil's Touch!!
So Listen To Me Listen Close
I Need A Favour Holy Ghost!!
Please Write This Message Make It Clear
That Evils Pay The Cash Is Fear!!
I'm Frightened Morning Noon And Night
I Have No Sword I Have No Fight!!
I Live Inside This Wicked Den

WHERE HITLER LIVES THE EVIL MEN!!
WE GNASH OUR TEETH YES IN THE NIGHT
OUR FLESH IS BURNING OFF A SIGHT!!
YOU'LL NEVER KNOW HOW BAD IT IS
THIS PLACE CALLED HELL, MY ADDRESS IS!!

JEWS

JEWISH TONGUES YOU HEAR THEM SAY
THERE IS NO GOD BUT OURS "THE WAY"!!
A TIME IT CAME THEN WENT IN PAST
A FAITH TRADITION BORN TO LAST!!
BUT NOW I'LL TELL YOU DARLING TRUTH
I'LL RAISE THEM UP TO GROW A PROOF!!
THE TIME HAS COME OH YES IT HAS
TO OPEN UP NEW GATES, A PATH
I'LL WALK THEM INTO BRAND NEW WAYS
THE GLORY COMES THE PRICE THEY'VE PAID!!
SO TWINKLE IN AND TWINKLE OUT
I'M BURSTING THROUGH TO SCREAM AND SHOUT!!
CAUSE BORING PRAYERS AND RITUALS HEAR
IT'S TIME TO TAKE OFF SHACKLES FEAR!!
CAUSE WHAT YOU DON'T KNOW YOU WILL SEE
I OWN THEM ALL THEY WORK FOR ME!!
I'VE GOT THEM PLANTED SPECIAL KNOW
TO TEST THE FAITH OF OTHERS GROW!!
SO DARLING WHISPER ME TO YOU
THE WORDS TO MAP THE PATHWAY THROUGH!!
YOU'LL WRITE SOME THINGS AND PUBLISH CLEAR
THE NEW BEGINNINGS TIME IS HERE!!
THE WORLD WILL BE SO HAPPY BRIGHT
IT'S TIME TO TAKE OFF VEIL TO LIGHT
A HEART THAT'S BURNING HOT WITH LOVE
A NEW POSITION FROM ABOVE!!

JESUS

John

NOTE: 5:05PM

His Soul told me that he walks and walks trying to find someone who can hear him. Then said some other souls told him to find me. Said I can hear and would pray him home. (Which I did).

I Live In Town And Walk Around
I Swam, I Dived, Then Drank Then Drowned
I Walk In Pubs And Clubs At Night
And Through The Day The Coffee's Right
I'm Not Sure Why I Can't Go Home
So Here I Am And Here I Roam
It's Not So Bad, I Like It Here
But Something Tells Me Not So Clear
That There's Another Place To Go
Where People See Me, Friends I Know!!
So Can You Help Me, Pray For Me
So I Can Go Be Truly Free??!!

Please Help Me. –John

Dominic Spirit in Hell!!

NOTE 4:50PM
IT WAS AN EERIE DAY, DARK CLOUDS, VERY WINDY. AS I GLANCED UP FROM THE BOOK I WAS READING, A POWERFUL GUST OF WIND BLEW BY. THE LEAVES WERE ROLLING THROUGH THE AIR WHEN I SAW ABOUT TWELVE SPIRITS MOVING IN THE WIND. THEY CAME IN AND LINED UP TO GIVE ME WRITINGS.

WAS VERY SCARY, BUT ALSO EXCITING!!

DOMINIC WAS STANDING IN FRONT OF ME, SAID HE DIED AT 24 YEARS OLD, HE WAS FROM LOS ANGELES, CALIFORNIA. HISPANIC MALE, SHORT BLACK HAIR WITH GEL, VERY HANDSOME, ABOUT 5'7". THIS IS WHAT HE TOLD ME.

I HAD A CAR I DROVE IT FAST
I SNORTED COKE THEN SPED THEN CRASHED!!
I LIVED A LIE MY LIFE ON EARTH
A SELFISH MAN ABANDONED BIRTH!!
I HAD SOME WOMEN AND CHILDREN SEE
WHEN FOUND THEM PREGNANT I'D ALWAYS FLEE!!
CAUSE FATHERHOOD WAS NOT FOR ME
JUST GETTING HIGH AND SEX FOR FREE!!
I PAVED A ROAD A HIGHWAY PATH
TO LOWER REALMS THE DEVIL'S LAUGH!!
THEY OWN MY SOUL I GAVE THEM KEYS
WHEN TRAPPING VICTIMS WAS ALL I BE
I GAVE THEM DRUGS I GOT THEM HOOKED
THEN TOOK THEIR LIFE THEIR POCKETBOOK!!
YOU SEE THE TARGETS THAT I HAD
WERE LITTLE CHILDREN MY GOD SO BAD

I Didn't Know The Penalty
Was Building Up My Sentencing
To Lower Places Lower Realms
Of Misery The Devil's Helms!!
The Ship Of Terror An Endless Trip
To Fear-filled Places Insane I R.I.P. (Reside In Pain)

Note: He showed me playgrounds where he would give drugs to children for free, get them hooked. Told them to steal from their parents to come back and buy the drugs.

Steven Surfer Dude Spirit

Note: 3:20pm

My Name Is Steven I Look Around
I See You Writing Without A Sound!!
Your Blazing Pen It Sees Us Bright
We're Walking In A Ghostly Sight!!
My God I Walked So Far So Fast
To Get To You To Give You Cash!!
Cause Money's In The Things You Write
A Trail Will Blaze And Give Us Sight!!
I Travel To The Lower Realms
And Guide Souls Through To Portals Helms!!
Cause Ships They Sail From Terror Fright
And Planes They Fly To Higher Heights!!
I'll Tell You Once I'll Tell You Twice
I've Come To Give You Peace Advice!!
The Troubled Souls You Lead Them Through
The Pearly Gates A Life Anew!!
But What You Need To Know My Dear
Is Payments Coming Its Day Is Near!!
So Please Remember Make It Quick
The Souls All Love Your Writings Schtick!!
Cause Faith Belief Is What You Give
It's Breath Of Heaven That You Live!!
So Tell You Something Tell You Close
This Peace Inside's From Holy Ghost!!
For Fountain Lives Inside Your Soul
For All To See And All To Know!!
The Love Of God Is Coming Fast

To Fill The Earth With Healing Blast!!
So Listen To The Words We Say
And Gently Pave The Path The Way!!
Cause One Day Stars Will Shine Real Bright
And Bring The World To Heaven's Light!!

CIVIL WAR MAN

NOTE: 2:32PM (WANDERING SOUL)
FRIEND OF MINE GAVE ME A CIVIL WAR BULLET AND AN
ABRAHAM LINCOLN DEATH MASK. HE WANTED ME TO KEEP
THEM FOR A COUPLE OF WEEKS AND SEE IF SOMETHING
WOULD MANIFEST FOR ME. WELL, IMMEDIATELY WHEN HE
PUT THE BULLET IN MY HAND I STARTED SEEING CIVIL WAR
SOULS, STANDING OUTSIDE THE WINDOW.

I NOTICED SOME LADIES WITH UMBRELLAS AND BIG
HOOP SKIRTS, HATS, DRESS STYLE FROM THE LATE 1800S
AND MEN WEARING CIVIL WAR UNIFORMS. AS I SAW THEM
I STARTED TO CRY. I HAD OVERWHELMING EMOTION WELL
UP INSIDE OF ME.

WHEN I SAT DOWN TO WRITE, A FEW OF THE SOULS
CAME IN AND SPOKE TO ME. CIVIL WAR MAN WAS SITTING
BY MY DESK WEARING A GREY UNIFORM.

HE SAID:
I FOUGHT A WAR I LIVED IN LAND
DEPLETED SOIL, POSITIONED, RAN
THE ANGRY BUNCH IT WAS OUR LOT
SO TIRED WORN, THIS FIGHTING COST!!
SO WON'T YOU PLEASE, PLEASE PRAY FOR ME
I WALK IN ANCIENT TIME YOU SEE
A TIME WHEN HORSES BUGGY'S RULE
A TIME WHEN BLACKSMITH WAS OUR TOOL!!
HE HELPED OUR HORSES AND WAGONS TOO
HE MADE US WEAPONS A COUNTRY NEW!!
YOU SEE A MAN HE HAD TO DIG
UNEARTH A LIFE TO TRULY LIVE

I WALK THE STREETS YES WATCH YOU DEAR
THE SKIN TIGHT CLOTHES AND MASKS YOU WEAR!!
YOU SEE WE WORKED AND PLANTED FIELDS
OUR LIVES WERE ROUGH OUR HEARTS WERE FILLED!!
WE HONOURED MARRIAGE, WE HONOURED LIFE
A RECIPE TO THRIVE DELIGHT!!
SO LET ME TAKE TO THIS PLACE
A TIME BACK WHEN DIVISIONS RACE!!
WE THOUGHT THE BLACK MAN WAS A DOG
A PET TO CARE FOR HOUSE AND FARM!!
WE USED HIM FARMING FIELDS AND MORE
WE USED THE WOMEN COOK AND WHORE!!
SO I MUST TELL YOU, I MUST SAY
WE BROKE SOME LAWS A SINFUL WAY!!
SO NOW I PAY THE PRICE I LIVE
ON SCRAPS OF FOOD FROM GARBAGE BIN!!
I'D GIVE IT ALL BACK NOW I KNOW
THE PENALTY THE PRICE TAG SHOWS!!
YOU SEE THE DEBTS I HAVE ARE LARGE
ETERNALLY I'M AT A LOSS!!

PLEASE PRAY FOR ME PLEASE!!
HELP ME PLEASE!!

Abraham Lincoln – Soldiers

Note: 1:25pm

Possibly You'll See The Signs
The Civil War A Fighting Time
A Hill Was Fought On Oh, One Day
The Men Were Shot And Died, They Stay
You'll Hear Them Whisper In Your Ear
And Strike A Special Cord Of Fear!!
You'll Get The Shivers Tremble Shake
As Men Walk Through Your Body, Quake!!
The Energy They Feed Off, Fuel
Is Hidden In You, Human Tool!!
You See We Need A Charge, Some Life
Is Hidden In Your Hearts Alight!!
So Don't Be Scared Just Walk On Through
You'll Bless The Souls That Stuck To New!!

Abraham Lincoln

NOTE: 3:17 PM
HAD BEEN GIVEN A CIVIL WAR BULLET AND LINCOLN DEATH
MASK FOR A LITTLE WHILE. LOTS OF CIVIL WAR VISITATIONS.
ON THIS DAY ABE WAS HERE. THIS IS WHAT HE SAID.

TECHNICALLY I FOUGHT A WAR
IT HAD TO DO WITH CIVIL CAUSE!!
THE TIME TO FIGHT WAS RIGHT BACK WHEN
THE BLACKS WERE CAGED AND SLAVED LIKE HENS!!
BUT DON'T YOU SEE IT WASN'T RIGHT??!!
THE ATMOSPHERE WAS LOW ON LIGHT!!
SO I BECAME THE GUIDING KNIGHT
TO BRING DIVISION, ONE UNITE!!
CAUSE SEPARATION WAS AT HAND
I BROUGHT TO STATES A WEDDING BAND!!
HAD MARRIAGE IN MY MIND YOU SEE
A POWER FORCE ALIVE AND FREE!!
FOR KNOW TO MAKE THE EAGLE FLY
THE WINGS MUST MEND TO HIT THE SKIES!!

LOVE TO YOU ALL!!

ABRAHAM LINCOLN

Sharon-Spirit

Sharon came to me at work and said this to me.

Write It Fast I Have No Time
The Clock Is Ticking, Yes On A Dime!!
I Lived, I Fought, I Died, I Crashed
A Drunken Mess, A Short Life Last!!
To Fix This Mess I Needed God
To Love Me Clean, Accept My Flaws!!
The Church I Went To Had A Claus
"You Must Be Perfect, Obey Our Laws"!!
But I Must Tell You This I Know
A Broken Wing Needs Love To Grow!!
I've Fallen Down So Many Times
Seems Life On Earth Was Pain-filled Crime!!
So I Must Say and I Must Show
My Life Was Hard And To Hell I Go!!
But Someone Caught Me When Falling Fast
Into The Pit Where Fires Blast!!
His Name Was Jesus Christ, I Know
Cause Skin Was Light It Had a Glow!!
He Pulled Me In His Arms You See
And Kissed Me With His Love!! Was Free!!!
I Filled With Light, A Soul Transformed
In Golden Gown, A Crown Adorned!!
He Told Me Once He Told Me Twice
I Was So Precious In His Sight!!
I Felt His Love Flow Through My Arms
I Sprouted Wings, He Healed My Harms!!
Yes Fly To Heaven This I Did

Was Filled With Angels, Thoughts Forgive!!
My Message This My Message Clear
Release To God All Angst and Fear!!
Cause It Will Bring You Far, Yes Down
And Strip Your Royal Garments, Crown!!
So Listen To Me, Listen Close
We Need To Ask The Holy Ghost
To Guide Us To His Pearls His Truths
And Let Us Walk In Higher Proof!!

God Is So Good!!!

Sharon In Heaven!!!

Elvis Presley

Note: 2:30pm

This Man He Came To Earth One Day
He Had A Thing Or Two To Say!!
He Shook, He Sang, He Danced Around
He Filled The World With A New Sound!!
I Sent Him Down From High Above
To Reach Across The Races Love!!
He Flew In Planes And Drove In Cars
And Broke Through Social Taboos' Laws!!
Cadillac He Drove It Pink
His Lifestyle Made The People Think
A Bad Boy Womanizer Was
But Special Mission Was His Cause!!
I Birthed Him Into Simple House
With Neighbours Black They Taught Him Shout!!
You'll Have To Know I'll Take A Stand
To Reveal Chosen Souls To Land!!
It's Time To Change The Church's Light
To Make It Colourful And Bright!!

Jesus

Angels, Saints, Jesus, Saint Joseph

Note: 1:18pm
At "Holy Grotto" in Oregon.

I Want To Tell You Secret This (Bless)
Your Knees Were Made For Wedding Bliss!!
When Kneeling To Your God In Three
A Strange Sensation Comes From Me
You See I Touch Your Soul With Love
A Heaven Dose To Lift You Up!!
I Want You Children Have No Fear
Just Loving Thoughts With Heart That's Clear!!
Cause Visions Blurred And Sometimes Blind
When Darkness Fills Your Heart And Mind
So Precious Darlings, Lambs, We Love
Prepare For Glory's Coming Cause
We'll Fill The World With Light So Bright
You'll Need Dark Glasses Day And Night!!!
Mother Mary/Angels

Guardian Angels!!

NOTE: 1:58PM
Angels told me this when I was at the "Holy Grotto"
in Oregon. (Had prayed At Grotto for four hours
after Mass, lots of messages.)

Angel Of God, My Guardian Dear
You Come With Love Release My Fear
You Watch Me Step In Places Dark
I Drift Off Path, In Thorns I Walk
One Day You'll Stop Me, Whisper Ear
And Take Me To A Pathway Clear!!
Will Be With Wisdoms Filled So Grand
And Hidden Keys To Treasured Plan!!

Trust Always In God's Goodness!!

Janis Joplin

NOTE: 4:38PM
JANIS WAS STANDING BY ME AND GAVE ME THIS WRITING. THE LORD HAD TOLD ME I WOULD GET A WRITING FROM JANIS FOR MONTHS. WELL, SHE FINALLY CAME AND SHE FINALLY SPOKE, SO HERE IS WHAT SHE SAID TO ME.

TOUGH WERE TIMES YOU KNOW BACK WHEN
A WOMAN'S LIFE WAS SERVING MEN
THE MOTHERS TAUGHT THE DAUGHTERS GLAD
LIVE HAPPY LIFE DON'T MAKE "HIM" MAD!!
JUST LISTEN CLOSE, YES GIVE HIM EAR
DON'T MAKE MISTAKE OR BEATINGS NEAR!!
A MAN WAS KING OF CASTLE THEN
A WOMAN'S LIFE WAS SERVANT HEN
A WRETCHED BARGAIN'S WHAT YOU GOT
WHEN HITCHED A RIDE ON DONKEY CART
YOU THOUGHT HE'D RIDE A STALLION FAIR
AND BRING YOU FLOWERS, PUT IN YOUR HAIR!!
BUT WHAT HE HAD IN MIND WAS WHORE
WHO'D WASH HIS DISHES SWEEP HIS FLOOR
BUT TIMES HAVE CHANGED SHE HAS A VOICE
AN EDUCATED MIND, A CHOICE!!
A MAN MUST EARN HER HEART HER TRUST
OR LEAVE HIM COLD, YES IN THE DUST!!

Sarah-In Heaven

NOTE: 1:06PM
SARAH CAME BACK. IN HEAVEN NOW.

I WALKED INTO A PLACE ONE DAY
I WALKED IN REALM SO DARK AND GREY
A SPECIAL SOUL SHE CARRIES SIGHT
SHE SAID A PRAYER AND TOOK MY FRIGHT!!
I ROAMED THE STREETS I WALKED AROUND
I SCREAMED IN CARS THEY HEARD NO SOUND
I PLEADED LOUD, "PLEASE HELP ME, PLEASE!!
UNLOCK THE CHAINS THAT BURDEN ME!!!"
AS FISH WILL SWIM AND DOGS WILL BARK
THERE WAS NO LIGHT THIS PLACE I WALKED
A TERROR FRIGHTENED WORLD I LIVED
I HAD THE GOLD BUT DID NOT GIVE!!
YOU SEE I PAID THE TICKET THERE
THE PRICE THE COST I DID NOT SHARE

SARAH

ALWAYS GIVE!!! ALWAYS LOVE!!!

BOB DYLAN

I SENT A MAN HIS SIZE WAS SMALL
HIS VOICE WAS BIG, UNIQUE, AND TALL!!
HE CAME TO EARTH A MESSAGE MAN
HE CAME TO FIGHT WITH PEN IN HAND!!
HE GATHERED SOULS TO FIGHT TO STAND!!
THEY SANG ALONG THE POWER GRAND!!
I'VE OPENED DOORS YOU SEE WITH MIGHT
"THE MUSIC MAN" HIS LIGHT SO BRIGHT!!
ILLUMINATE THIS WORLD OF OURS
TO STOP THE KILLING END THE WARS!!
A PROPHET YES HE IS THIS SOUL
HIS WORDS ARE RICH YES FILLED WITH GOLD!!
I WANT TO TELL YOU WRITE THIS DOWN
THROUGH MELODIES WE'LL LIFT THE GROUND!!
YES, RISE THE EARTH TO HIGHER PLACE
THAT'S FILLED WITH LOVE AMAZING GRACE!!

JESUS

Kurt Cobain

Written 6:43 am

My Name Is Cobain, Kurt You Know
I Walked In Simple Dress To Show!
I Twisted Thoughts Of Rock You See
No Makeup Man Or Glam For Me!!
I Sang Some Songs, Yes Pain In Tow
The Lessons In The Life I Know!!
This Suicide The Way I Died
It Made The World, The People Cry
You See The Homeless Poor, You Know
The Guitar Man In Grunge Will Show
A Love For Life, A Love For Man
Was How I Rolled My Rock My Stand!!

Love, Kurt

Jesus

Note: 12:59pm

Totally You Know I'm Yours
This Kingdom Has A Gift Of Doors!!
To Open Them You Need A Key
It's Made Of Love And Charity!!
The Master Locksmith Has A Plan
To Open Every Door To Man!!
Perfectly You Know I'll Tell
A Little Secret Place I Dwell!!
I Live In Mansions, High Rise Homes
And In The Ghettos There I Roam!!
You See The Hungry, Needy, Poor
Are Special Friends That I Adore!!
I'll Tell You Once I'll Tell You Twice
Must Help The Hurting, Heal Their Life!!
The Kingdom's Gates Will Open Wide
And Fill Your Life With Joy-filled Prize!!

Love My Angels!!

Love The Poor!!

Jesus

GEISHA-ARTIST

NOTE: 12:21PM
HAVE GEISHA WOMEN STANDING ALL AROUND ME (FROM
HEAVEN) SPEAKING TO ME, THIS IS WHAT THEY SAID.

A NUN SHE WEARS HER HABIT LOUD
IT MAKES HER WALK REAL TALL AND PROUD!!
SHE CARRIES GRACE AND DIGNITY
A WHITEWASHED FACE FOR ALL TO SEE!!
I'LL TELL YOU THIS I LOVE THE MOST
SHE BLESSES MAN A HOLY HOST!!
SHE MAKES HIM FEEL ALMIGHTY STRONG
AS SERVES HIM TEA AND KNEELS SO LONG!!
A KIND OF ROOM I HAVE A VIEW
SHE'S POURING BLESSINGS LOVE AND DEW!!
A GENTLE ANGEL IS THIS LASS
SHE LIFTS HER CULTURE BRINGS HIGH CLASS!!

SERVANTS THE LOWEST IS THE HIGHEST!!

GEISHA POWER SERVANT!!

HIGH FROM HEAVEN RARE TO REALM!!

HEALING POWERS FROM ONE LOOK STARE!!

LIFTS YOUR SOUL THIS WOMAN ON HER KNEES!!

THE LOUVRE

NOTE: A FEW DAYS BEFORE I WENT TO LONDON AND PARIS THIS WRITING CAME IN. AFTER SEEING THE MONA LISA AND BEING IN THE "PALAIS DU LOUVRE" I UNDERSTOOD WHAT THIS WRITING MEANT.

THE LOUVRE IT HAS A HISTORY RARE
THE PRINCES, KINGS, THE QUEENS THEY SHARE
A SPIRIT SPACE, A SPIRIT STAND
A POWER SPOT WITH ART THAT'S GRAND!!
I'LL TELL YOU THIS I'LL TELL YOU FAST
THE LOUVRE IT HAS A POWER BLAST!!
THE WINDOWS DOORS IT'S FILLED WITH LIGHT
THE ANGELS FLY THROUGH DAY AND NIGHT!!
I'LL WHISPER TO YOU THIS I WILL
THE MONA LISA HAS POWER SPILL!!
JUST DARE TO WALK AND LOOK IN EYES
A POWER JOLT WILL BE SURPRISE!!
WE'VE LEFT HER THERE WITH POWER STRONG
THE CENTURIES LOVED SHE HOLDS IT LONG!!
SO LOOK WITH ANGEL'S EYES AND KNOW
THE MANY PLACES LOUVRE WILL GROW!!

"BRING THE SPIRIT OF THE LOUVRE HOME WITH YOU AND YOU WILL BE BLESSED!!"

LEONARDO DA VINCI

Cat Stevens

Note: 5:05pm
Cat Stevens changed his name when he converted to Islam to "Yousef Islam". He had been a very famous singer/song writer before his conversion. Had been with a Friend who asked me if I Might Get A Writing On Cat Stevens. Well, the Lord touched me and said I would. A couple hours later the writing came in, so here it is.

Yousef Islam Was Chosen See
To Build A Bridge Of Love For Me!!
He Left A Life Of Wealth And Fame
To Learn About A Higher Plane!!
We Had This Planned Before His Birth
To Open Eyes To Islam Earth!!
Cause Hidden In This Land
Is Precious Golden Lamb!!
The Sacrifice Is Plain To See
A Culture Bowing On Their Knees!!
Must Fall And Worship On The Ground
To Grow A Faith Where Love Abounds!!
Someday We'll Open All The Vaults
And Lift The Veil To All The Walks!!

Jesus

Sir Laurence Olivier

Note: Sir Laurence Olivier is considered possibly the greatest actor of this century. He was here, standing near me very, very, strong.

I Love The Way You Say My Name
Sir Laurence Yes Olivier!!
I Watch You Write I Watch You Speak
Though Silent Here Allowed No Speech!!
A Realm You Live On Earth This Year
Is Changing Fast Becoming Clear!!
The Gates Will Open Up Yes Wide
A Longer Life And Health Will Thrive!!
We Want To Tell You Scream Yes Shout
The Coming Era's All About!!
But Mystery It Has To Be
Just Little Whisper Comes From Me!!
I Have A Message Loud Yes Clear
But Have To Blur It Fuzz It Hear/Here!!
You Think I Might Be Riddle Man
But Plainly Speaking Ain't So Glam!!
We Want To Prove You Hear Us High
So Doubt Will Leave As Writings Fly!!

Love, Laurence

John Denver

NOTE: 4:54PM
ON MY WAY TO LONDON, ENGLAND AND PARIS, FRANCE. AT THE AIRPORT IN CALGARY, ALBERTA CANADA DURING SEVEN HOUR LAYOVER. HAD JUST BOUGHT A NEW JOURNAL AND WAS SITTING DOWN WHEN JOHN DENVER SHOWED HIMSELF STANDING NEXT TO ME. SAID HE WANTED TO GIVE ME A WRITING. THIS IS WHAT HE SAID.

HOWDY THERE I LOVE YOU SO
A CORNY MAN I WAS I KNOW
BUT JULIE DARLING THINGS I SAY
INSPIRE YOU A DIFFERENT WAY!!
I HAD A WIFE CALLED ANNIE KNOW
MY LOVE FOR HER WAS TENDER GROW!!
WE LIVED ON MOUNTAIN AIR SO HIGH
AND SMOKED SOME POT SO WE COULD FLY!!
YOU SEE SOME DRUGS I DID THEM MUCH
BUT HEROIN I DID NOT TOUCH!!
A CAUTIOUS MAN I TRIED REAL HARD
TO LIMIT DRUGS AND DRINK TO YARD!!
CAUSE OUTSIDE GATED FENCE YOU SEE
THE PEOPLE HAD PERCEPTION ME!!
THEY THOUGHT THAT I WAS KIND AND FAIR
BUT WICKED SOMETIMES MADE ME FLARE!!
THE DRUGS AND DRINK INFLUENCED BAD
WOULD TAKE MY MIND AND DRIVE ME "MAD"!!
SO WRITE THIS FOR ME WILL YOU LOVE

MUST PURIFY MY SOUL BECAUSE
A SOUL CAN'T FLY OR OPEN WINGS
WHEN FILLED WITH LIES AND WEBS THAT CLING!!
A FREEDOM COMES WHEN WE COME CLEAN
AND GLORY BELLS ARE SONGS WE SING!!

JOHN

WALK IN TRUTH ALWAYS!!

JACK THE RIPPER

NOTE: 10:32AM
WRITING CAME IN WHILE I WAS TAKING A SHOWER. SAW YOUNG QUEEN VICTORIA AND PRINCESS DIANA IN MY LIVING ROOM. TURN OF THE CENTURY PROSTITUTES FILLED MY HOUSE. HEARD THEY WERE ENGLISH, FRENCH AND GERMAN.

(I HAD JUST COME BACK FROM LONDON AND PARIS THE WEEK BEFORE. HAD WALKED DOWN A STREET IN WHITECHAPEL WHERE THE JACK THE RIPPER TOUR IS. I HAD FELT SOULS OF PROSTITUTES ON THAT STREET PRIOR TO RUNNING INTO THE TOUR WHICH CONFIRMED MY FEELINGS.)

JACK THE RIPPER OH HE HAD
A HUNGER LUST TO KILL SO BAD!!
HE WALKED THE LONDON STREETS AT NIGHT
AND CAUSED THE WOMEN FEAR AND FRIGHT!!
A KNIFE HE WIELDED SLICED AND PARED
HIS VICTIMS POOR A CLASS THEY SHARED
HE TAUGHT THE WORLD TO LOOK AND KNOW
THE POVERTY THE WOMEN SHOW!!
SO MANY GIRLS THEY HAD NO CHOICE
NO ADVOCATE OR POWER VOICE!!
YES THROWAWAYS "THE LOWEST THINK"
BUT PRECIOUS SOULS ON STARVING BRINK!!
SEE MARTYRS ARE THESE PRECIOUS FEW
WHO SUFFERED DIED A STREET LIFE CREW!!
THE LESSONS TAUGHT THE LESSONS LEARNED

WE MUST RESPECT ALL LIFE AND BURN
WITH FLAMES OF HIGHER TRUTH AND CARE
FOR EVERY SOUL THE VALUE'S THERE!!

French Prostitutes

NOTE: 1:27PM
HAD COME BACK FROM PARIS, FRANCE THE WEEK BEFORE.
MY HOUSE HAD BEEN FULL OF PROSTITUTES' SOULS THE
DAY BEFORE AND THEY KEPT SHOWING ME THEIR WINGS
(WEARING GAUDY TURN OF THE CENTURY CLOTHING). WAS
READING WHEN THEY SHOWED THEMSELVES AND STARTED
SPEAKING.

AS PROSTITUTE OUR LIVES WERE DIM
BUT BRIGHT WITH MISERY AND SIN!!
THE CHURCH THEY SAID WE'D GO TO HELL!!
THEY JUDGED US LEFT AND RIGHT AS WELL!!
I THINK YOU KNOW WE'RE TELLING TRUTH
THE PAST IS OPEN FILLED WITH PROOF!!
THE MEN THEY TOOK US POUNDING THIGHS
TOLD US STORIES POURING LIES!!
SAID THEY'D TAKE US OUT OF HERE
BRING US COMFORTABLE NO FEAR!!
I'LL MAKE YOU SCREAM I'LL MAKE YOU SAD
I'LL STEAL YOUR SOUL AND DREAMS YOU HAD!!
THE ONES THAT WENT TO HELL YOU KNOW
WERE WICKED MEN WITH GOLDEN GLOW!!
THEY USED US, BEAT US, RAPED US HARD
DRUNKEN LUST WAS BUSINESS CARD!!
SO MANY LIVED ON FAMILIES DIME
THEY NEVER WORKED HAD IDLE TIME!!
SO FILLED THEIR DAY WITH LUST AND DRINK
PAINTED LADIES FOOD AND THINK!!
READ THE BOOKS AND PONDERED THOUGHTS

Argued Much In Coffee Shops!!
Heaven Knows We've Paid The Price
Worked The Streets Both Day And Night!!
Paved The Way For Heaven's Light!!
You See A Blazing Light Is Cast
When Suffer Much A Humble Class!!
Just Love Us Darling Julie Dear
And Fill Your Cup We Will With Cheer!!

The Working Girls

Jesus Knows All!! Sees All!! Know That!!

Note: Went to see Da Vinci Code Last Night.

Clear Your Vision Seems Today
As Winter's Leaves Fall Into May
The Sun To Rise Upon Your Dawn
As Winter's Skies Are Moved So Long.....
Into The Summer Comes A Plan
Renew The Face Of God To Man
As Mysteries Ravel To And Fro
Where Is Heaven's Kingdom Know
As Churches Come And Churches Grow
The Souls Give Up Don't Want To Go!!
As Fast It Seems So Light So Bright
But Then You See The Dark The Night!!
Of Sinful Preachers Filled With Greed
Must Keep Those Plates Filled For Their Need!!
To Help The Poor The Church Expense
But Watch Their Lives It Makes No Sense!!
The Polished Nails And Fancy Cars
Gives Jesus Christ A Face With Scars!!
They Represent Him Speak His Name
But Their Real Life It Is A Shame!!
To Speak Of God's Love In The Streets
And Sleep On Fancy Thread Count Sheets!!

Marriage

Ancient Laws And Ancient Ways
They Made The Man And Woman Stay,
But Times Have Changed There's Freedom And
A Different Light A Different Stand!!!

God Is Never Changing And Ever Changing!!

Gays Jesus

Nearly Never Do I Say
Jesus Christ Is Straight Or Gay
But Darling Dear I'll Tell You This
I Love A Man With Woman Twist
I Love His Dance I Love His Walk
I Love His Lisp The Way He Talks!!
But Don't You Know I Own Them All
The Big, The Fat, The Short, The Tall??!!
The Woman Brand I Love The Most
She's Strong, She's Butch, She's Big, And Bold!!
The Truth You SEE I Love Them All
The Gays, The Blacks, The Whites, The Golds
The Many Types Of People Moulds!!
So Don't You Worry Don't You Think
I Have A Plan, I'm WEDDING KING!!!!

Gays And Angels

Gays and Angels Blur The Lines
Between The Earth Between Divine
A Certain Type Of Soul This Is
That Lives A Life Of Sweet Forgive!!!
You'll Never Know The Truth The Love
I've Sprinkled On My SPECIAL DOVES!!

Jesus

ELVIS PRESLEY

NOTE: 3:29AM
WOKE UP WITH ELVIS STANDING BY MY BED.

ELVIS PRESLEY HAD DISGUISE
HE WORE IT WELL THE LADIES SIGHED!!
HE'D SHAKE A LEG AND SING,
A POWER IT WOULD BRING!!
BUT IF THE TRUTH BE KNOWN
HIS LIFE IS LESSONS SHOWN
TO LOVE YOUR HEART YOUR WIFE
IS MIRACLE DELIGHT
CAUSE IF YOU EVER DARE TO STRAY
YOUR JOY WILL GO AWAY!!!
THEN DRINK AND DRUGS WILL BE
YOUR "HAPPY" MISERY

Helen Keller

NOTE: 4:13PM
WAS WITH MY FRIEND WHO IS BLIND WHEN HELEN KELLER
REVEALED HERSELF. SHE SAID MY FRIEND'S SOUL GAVE ME
THE GIFT OF THIS WRITING.

HELEN KELLER HAS IN EYES
A SPECIAL LOOK A SOUL THAT'S WISE
SHE SOUGHT TO SHOW SHE SOUGHT TO GIVE
A BRAND NEW WAY FOR BLIND TO LIVE
SHE BROUGHT YES TOOLS INTO THIS LAND
SO SIGHTED SOULS WOULD UNDERSTAND
A HANDICAP IS DIFFERENT YES
BUT POSSIBLY A SPECIAL BLESS!!!

LOVE, HELEN

Dominic Visit From Hell!!

Note: 11:28am
Dominic came back. He was begging me to take this writing. His hair was Flame red, then turned yellow. Not sure what that means. When he came to me the first time he had dark brown hair. Very handsome, 24 year old Hispanic male.

I'm Dominic You Have To Know
I've Had A Life In Hell Below!!
I'm Out Right Now To Tell You This
My Life Was Hard A Poor Exist!!
I Followed Men I Had In Life
They Showed Me Drugs And Got Me High!!
As Little Child Understand
I Had Some Dreams I Had A Plan
I'd Fly In Jets I'd Walk On Air
As Astronaut My Life Was There!!
But Didn't Happen Know That Way
The Prison Life Was How I Played
A Jail Was House For Many Years
My Family There Were Crooks And Fears!!
So Listen Julie Understand My Plight
My World That Made This Man (Me)
(So Sad Dominic)

King Henry The Eighth

NOTE: 3:00PM
I WAS WITH MY FRIEND AND SHE SAID SHE THOUGHT IT WOULD BE INTERESTING IF I RECEIVED A WRITING FROM HENRY THE EIGHTH WITH ANNE BOLEYN OR SOMETHING OF THAT NATURE. I TOLD HER I FELT THEY WOULD GIVE ME A WRITING SINCE SHE ASKED. WELL, A COUPLE OF HOURS LATER THEY SHOWED THEMSELVES. HENRY AND ALL OF HIS WIVES WERE STANDING IN FRONT OF ME.

HENRY, YES YOU KNOW I AM
I LIVED IN TIME WHEN PAIN WAS GLAM!!
I CHOPPED SOME HEADS I STABBED A FEW
MY GREAT REWARD IS HISTORY VIEW!!
MY DAUGHTER MARY OH SHE HAD
A FIERCE DEVOTION RELIGION BAD!!
SHE SLAUGHTERED MUCH SHE THOUGHT WAS FINE
TO FOLLOW POPE HER RIGHT DIVINE!!
MUST KNOW MY HEART AND SOUL WAS THERE
WHEN ANNIE BOLEYN HAD AN HEIR!!
THE WORLD WAS DARK AND SOMEWHAT DIM
TO SEE A SAINT ELIZABETH!!
SHE LIFTED VEIL YES FROM THEIR EYES
TO KNOW A WOMAN COULD BE WISE!!
IMPORTANT YES MY DAUGHTER WAS
TO BUILD A HEART FOR WOMAN CAUSE!!
SO SPECIAL WAS HER SOUL
IT FIT RIGHT IN WAS MADE OF GOLD!!

GOD BLESS ALL WOMEN!!
HENRY

Jacqueline Kennedy Onassis

Note: 7:50pm
Was with my Friend when Jackie came in. Every time I'm with this Friend, the Kennedy's are with her for some reason. This is my first "Writing" from Jackie!! Very exciting because I Love Her!!

Jackie, Jackie, Yes I Am!!
A Special Gift From God To Man!!
I Had A Dress I'd Like To Wear
A Pillbox Hat Put On My Hair!!
You See And Know I Had A Class
To Teach The World Fill Life With Blast!!
I Married Men With Power Names
It Brought Me Much, It Brought Me Fame!!
But What The People Saw The Most
Was Graciousness A White House Host
I Brought A Grace Into The Land
So All The World Would Say "How Grand!!".
A Princess Yes, You know I Was
In Politics The Circle Of!!!

Note: She was showing me how she lifted up the White House and America in the eyes of the World as graceful and elegant (Set the bar for other First Ladies).

Anne Frank

NOTE: 2:44PM.
ANNE WAS AT MY WORK THE DAY BEFORE AND SAID SHE
WOULD GIVE ME A WRITING. I WAS READING A BOOK
WHEN ANNE FRANK STOOD IN FRONT OF ME AND STARTED
SPEAKING. I FELT VERY EXCITED, HADN'T SEEN HER SOUL IN
A WHILE.

THINK I AM A LITTLE GIRL
MOSTLY I'M AN ANGEL PEARL!!
LIVED A LIFE YES HERE ON EARTH
MOSTLY HAPPY MOSTLY WORTH!!
MOTHER FATHER THAT I HAD
LOVED ME MUCH AND MADE ME GLAD!!
AS YOU KNOW THE HISTORY SHOWS
WORLD WAR TWO HAD POWER BLOWS!!
HIT US HARD THE FACE OF JEWS
TAUGHT US MUCH THE LIFE WE KNEW!!
NEVER WOULD I EVER THINK
MISERY THE END WOULD BRING
SUFFERING A GOLDEN RING!!!
SEE MARTYRDOM IT BROUGHT US MUCH
HEAVENLY AN ANGELS TOUCH!!!
ALL OF US ARE SO HIGH THERE
HEAVENLY CAUSE GOD IS FAIR!!!
POWER BLESSINGS I WILL BRING
SAY MY NAME AND ANGELS SING!!!

LOVE, ANNE

WE ALL SURVIVED THE HOLOCAUST!!!

Adolf Hitler

NOTE: 3:10PM
WAS WITH MY FRIEND TODAY AND HE TOLD ME THAT MY
FRIEND OPENED THE DOOR FOR HIM TO COME. SHE IS A
BEAUTIFUL EAST GERMAN WOMAN.

I AM A MAN YOU KNOW MY NAME
KILLING MUCH WITH TORTURE FAME!!
I HAD A THIRST FOR BLOOD YOU SEE
THE JEWS THE GAYS THEY HATED ME!!
I'LL TELL YOU THIS I'LL TELL YOU QUICK
THE STORIES TOLD I'LL BURN YOUR WICK!!
THE FLAMES YOU SEE THE LIVING FIRES
ARE MARTYRDOMS OF SLAVES FOR HIGHER!!
MUST KNOW MUST THINK I'M BURNING BAD
IN LOWER PLACE MY SOUL IS AT!!
I LIVED A LIFE YES HERE ON EARTH
CONTROL I THRIVED THE WAR I BIRTHED!!

TORTURE!! TORTURE!!! HELL!!! HELL!!! HELL!!!!

Adolf Hitler

Note: 8:44pm
Just laid down to take a nap. Started to doze off when this writing came in. Jumped up to write it. Can't see him, but know he is here. (Don't want to see him, scary!!)

This Dusty Musty Place I Live
Is Filled With Creeps And Anger Rifts!!
The Paint Is Thinner On The Walls
The Ghost And Ghouls Walk Through The Halls!!
I'd Give It All The Life I Lived
To Sacrifice The Poor I'd Give!!
I Wish That I Could Turn Back Time
Repair My Sins My Mortal Crimes!!
I Dug A Hole So Deep I Live
You'll Never Know The Terror This!!
See Terror Never Sleeps At all
My Mind Is Filled With Crimes I Caused!!
So Tell The People Warn Them True
You Pay For All The Things You Do!!
The Price Is High There Is No Bail
For Place I Live My Address Hell!!
Please Warn The People

(Said released from Hell to give me writing)

CELINE DION

NOTE: 3:10AM
WAS KNEELING PRAYING WHEN THIS WRITING CAME IN,
ON MY WAY TO CLIMB IN BED. (SO TIRED)

I GAVE HER TO YOU YES WITH VOICE
SO LARGE SO SWEET A WOMAN CHOICE!!
SHE HAS A HEART SO CRYSTAL PURE
HER SONGS OF LOVE BELIEVE HER SURE!!
WE DROPPED HER WINGS SO COULD NOT SEE
SHE IS AN ANGEL SHE BELONGS TO ME!!
BUT I MUST TELL YOU ALL THE TRUTH
SHE FLIES SO HIGH EVERY NOTE'S THE PROOF!!

JESUS LOVES CELINE!!

Saint Queen Elizabeth The 1st

Note: Was kneeling praying on carpet near kitchen when I looked up and saw King Henry The Eighth in my doorway with some women. Tried to ignore that he was here as I am very tired and must get up early for church in the morning. Had just crawled into bed when I saw Queen Elizabeth standing next to my bed. She asked me if I would get up and receive this writing for her (she was very polite, kind).

Elizabeth You Know That's Me
I Have A Soul That Can Set You Free!!
You See I Come From High You Know
A Place Of God With A Heaven Glow!!
My Time On Earth Was A Power Place
To Lift The Thoughts Of The Human Race!!
An Era When She Seemed To Be
A Second Class Know A Woman Me!!
So When You Say My Name I'm "Hear"
Filled With Blessings Love And A Type Of Cheer!!
Just know I Have A Special Power
Surging Through My Veins That I Want To Shower!!

Love To You All!!

Saint Queen Elizabeth The 1st

MARRIAGE

NOTE: 4:43AM

A MAN CAN LOVE HIS WIFE SO MUCH
BUT HAVE DESIRE NOT TO TOUCH
CAUSE SOMETHING'S IN HIS HEART THAT SAYS
STAY WITH HER BUT GO AWAY
SEE SOUL CAN TRAVEL VERY FAR
NEEDS NO WHEELS KNOW NEEDS NO CAR
CAUSE SPIRIT LEAVES A MARRIAGE FAST
WHEN LOVE AFFAIRS ABORTED CRASHED!!
I THINK I WANT TO SAY THIS WRITE
TRUE LOVE MUST COME FROM GOD IGNITE
CAUSE IF THE LOVE OF GOD'S NOT THERE
THE SHIP WILL SINK WILL GO NOWHERE!!
SO I WILL TELL YOU THIS I KNOW
THE HEART MUST LIVE ON LOVE TO GROW!!
FOR IF IT ISN'T FED THIS TOUCH
YOUR LIFE WILL DIM IN DARKNESS MUCH!!

LOVE MEANS EVERYTHING!!

Father Francis

NOTE: 8:30PM

Was in Phoenix staying at my friend's house. Had laid down to rest and saw so many souls in his beautiful home. Had fallen asleep for a few minutes. As I woke up I saw a Catholic Priest sitting at a desk at the end of my bed. He was writing and he told me his name was Father Francis.

He wore turn-of-the-century priest garments. Had brown hair with lots of grey in it, also had a beard and wore glasses. He gave me a writing a few hours later.

Possibly You Know I Am
A Visitor At Night I Stand
So Near Your Bed I Stare And Walk
Right Through The Walls Know Doors Have Locks!!
If Truth Be Said And Truth Be Known
I Love This House And Call It Home
Cause Little Do The People Say
"Away From Me Must Keep At Bay!!"
I Am A Priest From Long Ago
This House Of Prayer Is Where I Go
Cause Many Souls From Many Times
Walk Through These Doors To Heaven Find!!
I Help A Little, Say A Prayer
Tell Them God Is Good And Cares!!

Love, Francis

Steven Spirit

NOTE: 8:30 PM
Was in Phoenix, Arizona visiting my dear Friend. He took me for a walk showing me his neighbourhood. I told him I was so tired, I was desperate to take a nap. Had just flown into town a couple of hours earlier and thought I was tired from the flight but that wasn't it. I needed to spiritually see who lived in his Early Phoenix home.

Very interesting Nap. Immediately when I laid down a soul named Steven walked through the wall and told me he lived in the house. Then I saw Jonathan, Maxim, and a few other spirits but I don't remember their names. The souls were gay men. Maxim was from the seventies. I could tell from his clothing.

Here is what Steven said to me:

I'm In A Rush Must Talk Real Fast
I'm Standing Near A Hearing Lass (Girl)!!
You Came In House This Afternoon
Was So Excited Felt To Swoon!!
Cause See Your Angel Wings You Wear
So Bright And Shiny Power Glare!!
We All Could See You Had The Sight
To Hear Us Clear So Bright Your Light!!
Know Souls Came Running Here To See
This Angel Girl Named Julie Be!!
I'm Going To Tell You Crystal Clear

70

A Thing Or Two I'll Whisper Ear!!
You Drive Us Wild The Things You Say
A Rock Star Of The Spirit Way!!

We All Love You Julie!!
Steven

Dalai Lama

NOTE: 4:54AM
HAD GONE TO CHINATOWN TO GET A MASSAGE LAST NIGHT.
AS I WAS BEING MASSAGED I KEPT SEEING BUDDHIST MONKS
SURROUNDING ME. SO MANY BUDDHIST WRITINGS WERE
BEING SPOKEN TO ME. I SAW THE CURRENT DALAI LAMA
STANDING IN THE CORNER OF THE CHINESE MASSAGE
PARLOUR. HE HAD HIS HANDS TOGETHER AND KEPT BOWING
AND SMILING AT ME. JUST NOW DALAI LAMA AND BUDDHIST
MONKS WOKE ME UP TO GIVE ME THIS WRITING. MY HOUSE
IS FILLED WITH MEN AND WOMEN OF TIBET. I AM A LITTLE
OVERWHELMED RIGHT NOW.

A BUDDHIST MAN HAS SEALED HIS FATE
AS SPECIAL DOOR YES, SPECIAL GATE!!
A CHOSEN SOUL HE IS BECAUSE
DIVINITY'S INSIDE HIM LAWS!!
HE'S BOUND BY PRAYER HE'S BOUND BY GOD
TO SEND THE WORLD A PERFECT CAUSE!!
SO LISTEN TO THIS MAN DIVINE
FOR HAT IS HIGH HIS CHAIR SUBLIME!!
HE COMES TO EARTH TO GIVE US LOVE
A SPECIAL KIND SO HIGH BECAUSE
HE'S TIED UP TIGHT IN HISTORY
OF MANY PRAYERS AND POVERTY!!
CAUSE MAN WHO PRAYS AND HUNGERS MUCH
RECEIVES A CROWN OF GLORY TOUCH!!

JESUS LOVES BUDDHISTS

Patrick Swayze

NOTE: 3:35PM
WAS WITH MY FRIEND WHEN PATRICK SWAYZE SHOWED HIMSELF AND SAID HE WOULD GIVE ME A WRITING THROUGH THE BLESSING HER SOUL WAS GIVING ME. WELL, IT WAS THE NEXT DAY THAT HE CAME TO ME AND SPOKE, THIS IS WHAT HE SAID.

DESPERATELY YOU KNOW I AM
INSIDE THIS REALM THAT AIN'T SO GLAM
I SEE YOUR SOULS, THIS LIFE ON EARTH
WITH HUNGERS COLD NO HOMELESS WORTH
IT'S PLAIN TO SEE YOU'VE GOT THE CASH
TO HEAL THE WOUNDS AND HEAL THE RASH
OF CHILDREN PROSTITUTION THERE
A WORLD OF PEOPLE LITTLE CARE
SO I WILL TELL YOU THIS I WILL
A CHANGE IS COMING, A HOLY SPILL
OF HEAVEN'S LIGHT OF HEAVEN'S LOVE
TO HEAL WITH THOUGHTS ARE FROM ABOVE!!

NO MORE HUNGER!!

NO MORE WAR!!

NO MORE CHAOS!!

HEAVENS COMING TO EARTH HIGHER AWARENESS!! ACTION!!

LOVE, PATRICK SWAYZE

Robert Pattinson

NOTE: 3:20AM
HAVE HAD THE SOUL OF ROBERT PATTINSON IN MY HOUSE SINCE WEDNESDAY NIGHT AFTER I SAW "NEW MOON". HE CAME TO ME LAST YEAR MANY TIMES AFTER I WENT TO SEE THE TWILIGHT MOVIE AND TOLD ME SPIRITUAL INSIGHTS ABOUT THE PHENOMENON OF THE TWILIGHT SERIES. LAST YEAR I HAD SEEN SO MANY ANGELS COMING OUT OF THE MOVIE SCREEN. THIS YEAR, JUST FELT THE ANGELS COMING INTO MY SOUL GIVING ME A POWER CHARGE. SAW HIM IN MY HOUSE BEFORE I WENT TO SLEEP. HE JUST WOKE ME UP A BIT AGO TO GIVE ME THIS WRITING.

ROBERT IS STANDING NEXT TO ME RIGHT NOW (HIS ETERNAL SOUL). HIS SOUL IS THE SOUL OF AN ANGEL WHO CAME DOWN TO EARTH AT THIS TIME TO PLAY THE ROLE HE WAS BORN TO PLAY "EDWARD".

IN LOVE WITH ME I KNOW YOU ARE
AN ANGEL AM A SUPERSTAR!!
I'VE COME TO EARTH THIS TIME I LIVE
TO LIFT UP LOVE IS WHAT I GIVE!!
CAUSE LOVE HAS FALLEN DOWN SO FAR
IT SEEMS LIKE HATE THE LOWEST BAR!!
I WANT TO RAISE IT UP YOU SEE
INTO THE GATES OF HEAVEN BE!!
CAUSE WOMAN'S HEART WAS MADE TO SOAR
INTO THE HEIGHTS THROUGH HEAVEN'S DOOR!!
THE BURST OF HEAVEN THAT I BE
WILL FEED THE HEARTS OF ALL THE SHE'S!!

SO LISTEN TO ME LISTEN CLOSE
I'LL LIFT THE VEIL AND MAKE A TOAST
CAUSE RESURRECT YOUR HEART I WILL
AND HUNGER IT WITH POTENT THRILL!!
YOU'LL SEE A TIME IS COMING SOON
WHERE LOVE WILL LIFT YOU TO THE MOON!!

LOVE, ROBERT "EDWARD"

Brad Pitt

NOTE: 9:05AM
Woke up hearing this. Brad Pitt's Eternal soul was standing in my bedroom, then my living room when he gave me this writing.

I Came To Earth You Know I Did
With Special Mission That I Live!!
At First I Was A Glamour Man
Then Veil It Fell See Who I Am!!
A Purpose Life I'm Driven See
To Set The Hungry Captives Free!!
Cause Sick And Cold In Pain They Live
I Hate To See That's Why I Give!!
I Have To Keep Some Change In Jar
Cause Hollywood I Am A Star!!
But If The Truth Be Known Be True
I'd Give It All That's What I'd Do!!
So Look At Me And Open Eyes
Just Help A Little With Your Tithes
Cause Church Of Jesus Christ You See
Is Helping Those Who's Sick In Need!!

God Loves All People!!
All Races And Religions!!
Or Non Religions!!
Everyone!!
This Is The Truth!!

Love Brad

Amish Angels

Note: 9:30pm
Amish Angels had been in my dream. They were shouting praises to God singing "Sing Hallelujah To The Lord". Woke up and they were still in my room singing and rejoicing!! Had seen Flashes of Amish Angels all day then tonight they gave me a writing. Just woke me up right now again at 1:55am. I am very tired, sleepy.

An Amish Man Is Plain You See
He Has A Special Mission Me!!
I Sent Them There To Till The Soil
To Rid The Earth Of Fleshly Spoils!!
Cause Show To You, You Know He Will
A Simple Life He Takes No Pills!!
So Hard He Works Before The Light
And Comes Into His Home At Night!!
Resourceful Man He Is Because
A Simple Life With Hard Work Laws!!
So Darling Would You Plainly See
A Simple Tool The Amish Be!!??
They'll Show You How To Live In Joy
Without A Lot Of Worldly Toys!!

Hard Work!!
Honesty!!
Integrity!!
Family Love!!
Prayer!!
Jesus Loves The Amish!!

Julia Child

I CAME TO EARTH YOU KNOW I DID
TO LOOK AT LIFE TO LIFT THE LID!!
A WOMAN HAD NO RIGHTS BACK WHEN....
JUST LOOKING PRETTY SERVING MEN!!
I CAME TO LIFE IN EARTH A TIME
WHERE WOMAN HAD NO VOICE NO RHYME!!
SHE TRIED REAL HARD TO KEEP A WAIST
SO LITTLE THIN DON'T GAIN NO WEIGHT!!
BUT BROKE THE LAWS I DID BECAUSE
I'D BUTTER DISHES AS MY CAUSE!!
SEE WOMEN SERVED AND COOKED THE MEN
BUT HIGH RESPECT PRESTIGE NOT THEN!!
I TOOK THE FLOOR I TOOK THE KNIFE
I CHOPPED AND PARED AND PEELED AND SLICED!!
I COOKED THE WORLD I GAVE ADVICE
I SHOWED THE WOMAN MORE THAN WIFE!!

RESPECT I GAVE RESPECT I LIVED
MY STORY IS JUST WHAT I GIVE!!

CAME TO LIFT UP THE KITCHEN IN THE EYES OF MEN!!

LOVE,
JULIA

BRUCE LEE

NOTE: 5:54AM
WOKE UP AND SAW BRUCE LEE WALK IN MY FRONT DOOR.
HE LOOKED AT ME AND SAID "HELLO JULIE, I CAME TO GIVE
YOU A WRITING ON "THE DRAGON"!!

I CAME TO EARTH A CHINESE MAN
I CARRIED WHIP AND SWORD IN HAND!!
INVISIBLE YOU COULD NOT SEE
THE WEAPONS OF DESTRUCTION ME!!
I HAD A WIFE A CAR AND KIDS
BUT SECRETLY A SPIRIT LIVED
INSIDE MY SOUL INSIDE MY MIND
THE DRAGON FORCE WAS FRIEND OF MINE!!
SEE ASIAN CULTURES WE BELIEVE
THE DRAGON COMES THEN POWER BREATHES!!
THE DRAGON BRINGS IT FROM ON HIGH
THEY LIVE IN HEAVEN WHERE THEY FLY!!
SO LISTEN TO ME LISTEN NOW
TO LOVE THE DRAGON TAKE A VOW!!
YOU MUST RESIDE IN CHARITY
AND LOVE THE POOR WITH ALL YOU BE!!

DRAGON POWER-GIVE
DRAGON POWER-FORGIVE
DRAGON POWER-LOVE
DRAGON POWER-COURAGE

DRAGON POWER-TRUST
DRAGON POWER-FIGHT FOR TRUTH ALWAYS

LOVE,
BRUCE - "THE DRAGON"

Blind Angels

NOTE: 9:44AM
Last night had dozed off for about an hour when I woke up with a shock as there were about 10 Angels standing by my door. All of them had white cloths wrapped around their heads like a blindfold. They were wearing off white garments that looked like coarse material. After I saw them they told me to go back to sleep that they would give me a writing in the morning. When I woke up in the morning I saw them again for about a half an hour on and off. Finally they told me to come kneel down and pray and they would give me a writing, well here it is. (These Angels had a mysterious power to them, very intriguing!! I Love These Angels!!)

The Blind They See A Different Way
Care Not If Black Or Brown Or Grey!!
They Have A Look A Vision See
That Looks Within The Heart Of Thee!!
So Take Some Lessons Learn Them Quick
And Open Eyes To Light The Wick!!
For Heart Of Man Is Dark And Bare
So Many Eyes They Look And Stare!!
See Action Take They Do It Not
Their Soul Receives A Type Of Rot!!
To Be A Free And Happy Man
Must Live A Life Of Giving Hand!!!
If Hand Is Fist All Clenched Real Tight
Your Joy Will Leave And Fill With Fright!!

So Listen To The Angels Please
Respect The Poor The Sick In Need!!
The Power Life You Dream Of Might
Need Giving Hand To Turn On Light!!

Give!! Give!! Give!!
Joy!! Joy!! Joy!!
Peace!! Peace!! Peace!!

Love,
The Blind Angels

Brittany Murphy

Note: 3:24am
Woke up, looked at my phone, saw that my friend
had sent me a text that Brittany Murphy had died.
Well, I woke up hungry so was cooking some cereal
when she spoke to me in the kitchen and asked me
to write for her, so I did.
   (She is hanging out with Heath Ledger)

I Came To Earth I Soared I Flew
Untimely Death Breaks Open View!!
See Need To Know The Reasons Why
A Girl Like Me Would Have To Die!!
I Lived A Life Yes Here On Earth
Had Hopes And Dreams Some Lived Some Birthed!!
But Star It Faded Far Too Fast
My Short Career Had Lost It's Blast!!
So Sad Depressed My Life Became
I Had No Work No Fame To Claim!!
So Look Real Hard Lift Up Your Eyes
I'll Wink To You Where Angels Fly!!
Cause Live In Heaven This I Do
I'll Say Some Prayers Lift Up Your View!!

Love,
Brittany

BEAUTIFUL HERE!!

BACK HOME IN HEAVEN!!

LOVE TO ALL OF YOU!!!

RELEASE ANGER!! RELEASE FEAR!! LOVE!!

Cory Haim

NOTE: 8:15AM
HAD FOUND OUT THAT CORY HAIM HAD DIED. CAME HOME FROM WORK THAT NIGHT NOT THINKING ANYTHING ABOUT HIS DEATH. THEN WENT TO CLOSE THE BEDROOM WINDOW BEFORE GOING TO SLEEP. SAW HIM SMOKING A CIGARETTE PACING BACK AND FORTH IN FRONT OF MY BUILDING.

    THE NEXT MORNING 8:00AM SAW A FLASH OF HIM STANDING NEXT TO MY FRIDGE THEN STARTED HEARING HIM SPEAK THIS WRITING TO ME.

I LIVED A LIFE I LIVED IT FAST
I DID SOME DRUGS I DIDN'T LAST!!
I TRIED REAL HARD TO KICK I DID
BUT FELL APART THIS WILL I GIVE!!
SO SAY A PRAYER FOR ME YOU WILL
I'LL BE SENT HOME TO HEAVEN CHILL!!
I WALK AROUND SEE SOUL IN HARMS
THE NAKED TRUTH THE NAKED ARMS!!
CAUSE WHEN DO DRUGS YOU PAY A PRICE
OF PAIN-FILLED DEATH TAKE MY ADVICE!!
SO LET IT GO THIS LIFE YOU LIVE
WHERE HIGH'S THE GOAL TO HELLISH GIVE!!!

CORY

THANK YOU,

PLEASE PRAY FOR ME

SEND ME HOME

Bill Gates

NOTE: 12:34PM
WRITING CAME IN WHILE I WAS AT WORK, SAW A FLASH OF
BILL GATES STANDING BY MY DESK, THEN SAW A FLASH OF
JESUS STANDING BY THE WALL NEAR ME.

I BROUGHT HIM HERE YOU KNOW I DID
TO OPEN GATES SO POOR COULD LIVE!!
I GAVE HIM GRACES FROM ABOVE
TO OPEN EYES RAISE BAR OF LOVE!!
CAUSE WHAT HAS MEANING HIGHER TRUTH
IS POWER GIVING RAISE THE ROOF!!
SO KNOW THIS MANY EYES WILL STARE
AT GEEKY MAN WITH SLOPPY HAIR!!
I MADE HIM SPECIAL DON'T YOU SEE
TO CLOSE THE GAP THE POOR SET FREE!!

JESUS

RAISE THE BAR OF GIVING!!
OPEN EYES TO POOR!!
LOVE ONE ANOTHER!!
GIVE!! GIVE!! GIVE!!

WARREN BUFFETT

NOTE: WOKE UP AT 4:56AM WITH THE SPIRIT OF WARREN BUFFETT STANDING TO THE RIGHT OF MY BED, KEPT REPEATING THE FIRST COUPLE OF LINES OF THIS WRITING. HE TOLD ME "GET UP!! GET UP!! RECEIVE THIS WRITING!! RIGHT AWAY!!"

HE TOLD ME THAT IT IS EASIER FOR ME TO RECEIVE WHEN I FIRST WAKE UP. I WAS SO TIRED, DIDN'T WANT TO WAKE UP!!

EXECUTIVE YOU KNOW I AM
THIS IS THE TRUTH IT AIN'T NO SCAM!!
I CAME TO EARTH YOU KNOW I DID
WITH SPECIAL BLESSINGS BUSINESS GIVE!!
I ROCK THIS WORLD I ROCK IT RIGHT
INSPIRE THOSE TO SEE THE LIGHT!!
CAUSE LIGHT OF GOD IS IN MY HAIR
MY GLASSES SHOES THE CLOTHES I WEAR!!
THEY LOOK TO ME FROM NORTH AND SOUTH
THEY LOOK TO ME TO HELP THEM OUT!!
BUT DON'T YOU SEE I GUIDE THEM TRUE
TO PROSPER MUCH WITH GIVING VIEW??!!
WE MUST REPAIR THE RIGHTS THAT WRONG
LIFT UP THIS WORLD AND GET ALONG!!
SO GIVING HAND I'LL SHOW YOU MINE!!
YOU'LL FOLLOW ME WE'LL LIVE DIVINE!!

WARREN

Must Help The Poor!!

Heal The World-Give!!

Open Your Eyes To The Hurting!!

Help The Lonely, The Elderly, The Abandoned!!!

Princess Diana

NOTE: 8:07AM
WOKE UP. DIANA TOLD ME TO GET UP, TAKE THIS WRITING,
THEN GO TO THE GYM!! SAID IT WAS VERY IMPORTANT FOR
ME TO TAKE THIS WRITING FROM HER NOW!!
 (I HAD WANTED TO REST JUST A LITTLE MORE AS I HAD
BEEN AWAKE MOST OF THE NIGHT PRAYING. VERY TIRED.)

MY NAME'S DIANA DON'T YOU KNOW
I LIVE IN HEAVEN GOLDEN GLOW!!
I LIVED ON EARTH SO MEEK BUT LARGE
FULFILLED MY PURPOSE HAD A CAUSE!!
THE POOR THE PRINCESS THAT I BE
HAD SPECIAL EYES TO LOOK TO SEE!!
THE PAIN I SAW WAS EVERYWHERE
INSIDE THE THRONES BENEATH THE STAIRS!!
CAUSE POVERTY'S A SPIRIT SPACE
IT LIVES WITH YOU KNOW CAN'T ERASE!!
THE ONLY WAY TO MAKE IT WELL
RELEASE YOUR THOUGHTS TO JOYFUL DWELL
IS LOVE THY NEIGHBOUR LOVE THY WIFE
A GIFT YOU GIVE NOT ONCE OR TWICE!!
YOU LIVE A LIFE OF GIVING HAND
TO FREE YOUR SOUL MUST UNDERSTAND
CAUSE WEALTH BELONGS TO ALL YOU SEE
SO TEACH THE DULL SO BRIGHT CAN SEE!!

LOVE, DIANA

GIVE KNOWLEDGE -LOVE

GIVE WISDOMS -LOVE

GIVE RESOURCES -LOVE

GIVE TIME -LOVE

THOMAS JEFFERSON

NOTE: 8:41PM
HAD JUST CRAWLED IN BED, STARTED TO READ MY BOOK
WHEN I SAW A FLASH OF THOMAS JEFFERSON AT THE LEFT
SIDE OF MY BED, THEN SAW A FLASH OF JESUS AT THE FOOT
OF MY BED. HE WAS SURROUNDED BY BLACK WOMEN!!

HEARD THIS WRITING REALLY LOUD. RAN TO GET MY
BOOK TO WRITE IT IN BEFORE MESSAGE FADED AWAY.

HAD JUST BEEN WATCHING THE HISTORY CHANNEL,
PRESIDENTS OF AMERICA. SHOW MUST HAVE OPENED A
SPIRITUAL DOOR, I GUESS.

THOMAS JEFFERSON YOU SEE
HE BROKE SOME LAWS HE WORKED FOR ME!!
HE HAD A WIFE YOU KNOW HE DID
BUT MARRY HER HE WOULD NOT GIVE
A LOVE WAS TENDER A LOVE HAD BLOOM
MUST UNDERSTAND IN SERVANTS ROOM!!
SO LOSE YOUR JUDGEMENT HAVE TO DO
WHEN FOUNDING FATHERS GIVE NEW VIEW!!
CAUSE LOVE CAN NEVER BE THROWN OUT
A PRESIDENT WILL BRING IT CLOUT!!

JESUS

BROKE RACIAL BARRIER!!

ILLEGAL LOVE!!

UNSPOKEN LOVE!!

RACIAL UNION!!

Johnny Cash

NOTE: WOKE UP 12:48AM
JOHNNY CASH WAS STANDING ON THE LEFT SIDE OF MY BED
HOLDING AN ACOUSTIC GUITAR. THEN HE FLUNG IT ON HIS
BACK AS HE LEANED OVER TO TALK TO ME. HE KEPT ASKING
ME TO TAKE A WRITING FOR HIM. REALLY WANTED TO, BUT
FELT ALMOST COUNSELLED WITH EXHAUSTION. HE LOOKED
ABOUT 40 YEARS OLD, OF COURSE HE WAS WEARING ALL
BLACK!! FINALLY GRABBED A PEN AND TOOK THE WRITING,
HERE IT IS.

I CAME TO EARTH YOU KNOW I DID!!
SOME PETTY CRIME I DID AS KID!!
BUT PAIN IT BROUGHT ME OUT OF GOOD
AND MADE ME BLACK AS DARKEST WOOD,
WAS DRUGS AND DRINK I LIVED WITH PAIR
THEY TOOK ME INTO DEVIL'S LAIR!!
THE GRIP WAS STRONG I COULDN'T SEE
JUST HOW I HURT MY LOVE AND ME!!
CAUSE LIFE I LIVED WAS NEAR DESTROYED
AS DEVIL TOYS TOOK ALL MY JOYS!!
JUST WOKE TO TAKE ANOTHER HIT
OF COKE OR PILLS OR DRINK A BIT!!
A POISONED MAN I WAS YOU SEE
TILL JESUS CAME AND SET ME FREE!!
I LIVE WITH HIM IN HEAVEN NOW
JUST CAME TO GIVE YOU MESSAGE VOW!!
JUST GIVE YOUR LIFE TO HEAVEN SEE
THE ONLY WAY TO BE SET FREE!!

LOVE JOHNNY

Jimi Hendrix

NOTE: 1:30AM
JUST WOKE UP.

Jimi was standing by my bedroom door. Felt the urge to go on my knees to pray, looked up and saw a flash of him standing there, then started hearing him speak this writing to me.

Guitar It Cried So loud It Did
A Black Man's Soul It Bled It Bit!!
I Sunk My Teeth In Music Much
A Gentle Man With Mystic Touch!!
The Chords I Played They Flew Real High
An Ecstasy They'd Make You Fly!!
Cause Voice I Carried In My Song
Was Loudest Cry Of Racial Wrongs!!
I Opened Gates You Know It's True
A Samson Am Delilah Too!!
So Look At Me You Can You Will
You'll Understand My Language Feel!!
The Music Moves And Sets You Free
Of Hate Damnation Black Man Me!!

Love,
Jimi

John Lennon

NOTE: 10:29AM
A FEW DAYS AGO I STARTED SEEING GLIMPSES OF JOHN LENNON, KEPT HEARING "I WILL GIVE YOU WRITING SOON."

HAVE BEEN WANTING A WRITING FROM HIM FOR SO LONG. ABOUT TWO YEARS AGO HE CAME TO ME SEVERAL TIMES IN THE NIGHT, AWOKE ME AND TOLD ME SPIRITUAL TRUTHS. SAID THE SONG IMAGINE IS A PRAYER. AND THE MORE IT IS HEARD, PLAYED/PRAYED, SUNG, THAT THE SONG/PRAYER WAS ACTIVATED.

HAVE NEVER RECEIVED A WRITING FROM HIM UNTIL THIS MORNING. I LOOKED UP AND SAW JOHN LENNON, HE SAID "TAKE IT NOW, I CAN GIVE YOU WRITING NOW!!"

GRABBED A PIECE OF PAPER AND SCRIBBLED IT DOWN.

I'M POWER FULL YOU UNDERSTAND
MY NAME IS JOHN A BEATLE AM!!
WE CAME TO WORLD TO ROCK IT RIGHT
TO OPEN EYES TO EASTERN LIGHT!!
CAUSE MUSIC WAS OUR GLUE OUR BAIT
TO BRING TOGETHER SPIRITS!! RACE!!
DIVISION HAS TO GO AWAY
SO WALLS FALL DOWN A BRAND NEW DAY!!
WHERE LOVE EXPLODES FROM EVERY HEART
RELIGION DIFFERENCE IS AN ART!!
CAUSE HEAVEN LOVES YES EVERY MAN
I SEE IT CLEAR CAUSE GATES I'M IN
SO LISTEN TO ME LISTEN CLOSE
I'VE COME TO BLESS THROUGH HOLY GHOST!!
I LOVE HIM YES YOU KNOW I DO!!!

THIS JESUS SUPER STAR IS TRUE!!!
SO WALK WITH ME, YES WALK MY WAY
LET'S CELEBRATE THE WORLD LET'S PLAY!!

LOVE, JOHN

COMPLETELY LOVE ONE ANOTHER!!

LOVE THE DIFFERENCES!!

ALL COLORS OF GOD!!

ALL WE NEED IS LOVE!!!!

Sally Hemings (Slave)

Note: 8:41pm
Was taking a bath when I heard woman's voice (In the spirit). She started giving me a writing, got out of tub as soon as I could to take the writing before it faded away. She showed herself to me wearing maid uniform with white apron and a white maid's bonnet on her head. Said she was Sally Hemings, slave of Thomas Jefferson.

As soon as I got to book with pen, writing had faded, couldn't remember one word of it.

But still saw flashes of her standing by me.

After about five minutes she spoke again and this is what she said.

Sally Hemings Is My Name I Was A Maid
A Slave By Trade
I Loved A Man In White House See
At First He Just Molested Me!!
But Time Went By He Softened Much
He Cared A Bit With Gentle Touch
But Don't Mistake The Life I Had
Was Forced Entry Into My Bed!!
I Never Wanted Him To Share
My Privacy So Naked Bare!!
So Publicly I Want You Write
My True Confession Here Tonight
This Life I Lived A Time Ago
Had No Romance Just Used Then Go!!
So Write This For Me Please You Will

My Dignity Was Taken Ill!!
It Made Me Sick The Things He'd Do
As Little Girl He'd Rape Me Too!!
A Martyr's Life I Had To Live
A Shame Filled Life Of Sex "I'd Give"

Thank You

Sally

Raped Me

Used Me

Loved Me

Marilyn Monroe

NOTE: 3:30AM
MARILYN HAS NEVER GIVEN ME A WRITING BUT I GUESS
TONIGHT IS THE NIGHT (MORNING).
   SHE SHOWED HERSELF IN MY BEDROOM A FEW MINUTES
AGO SAID I NEEDED TO GET OUT OF BED AND TAKE WRITING
NOW!! FELT URGENT, SO THIS IS WHAT SHE SAID.

SO BEAUTIFUL YOU KNOW I WAS
INVINCIBLE TO BEAUTY'S LAWS!!
I BROKE THEM MUCH YOU KNOW I DID
AS SEXY SIREN WOMAN LIVED!!
A FAMOUS MAN I LOVED HIM MUCH
A PRESIDENTIAL KIND OF TOUCH!!
HIS BROTHER YES, I LOVED HIM TOO
THE "BOBBY GATE", HOTELS WERE FEW
BUT LISTEN JULIE WHAT I SAY
I PAID A PRICE FOR FAME SO GAY!!
MY HEART WAS BROKEN MANY TIMES
I BLED IN BED WITH TEARS DIVINE!!
JUST WANTED SAFETY LOVE FOR SURE!!
WITH CONFIDENCE A LOVE SECURE!!

LOVE, MARILYN

SO LONELY!!

SO MUCH PAIN!!

HAPPY NOW IN HEAVEN!!

Abraham Lincoln - Slaves

NOTE: 7:41AM
ABRAHAM LINCOLN WAS IN MY HOUSE LAST NIGHT, SAW THREE FLASHES FROM HIM. WOKE UP THIS MORNING, WAS PRAYING ON MY KNEES WHEN HE SHOWED HIMSELF STANDING NEAR THE KITCHEN. WRITING CAME IN LOUD!!

FOUNDING FATHERS ALL YOU SEE
MADE A MESS TO SET SLAVES FREE!!
DEPENDANT WAS YES ALL THE LAND
ON "DARKIE'S" HELP YOU UNDERSTAND!!
OUR ROADS AND RAILROADS HOMES AND FARMS
DEPEND ON MUSCLE BLACK MAN'S ARMS!!
I THINK YOU KNOW I'M DRAWING SEE
A NATION NOW DEPENDENT THEE??!!
CAUSE SLAVES YOU ARE TO OIL NOW
MUST PULL UP SHADES LET LIGHT IN THOU!!
CAUSE ATMOSPHERE IS GROWING BLACK
WITH CHEMICALS WE CAN'T HAVE THAT!!
SO CLEAN IT UP I KNOW YOU WILL
SO WORLD IS CLEAN SO FRESH AND CLEAR!!

LOVE, ABE

WE WILL FOREVER WATCH OVER OUR LAND!!

George Washington

Note: 8:15am
Was trying to walk out the front door. Felt energy drop me to my knees, then saw George Washington (flash of him), immediately this writing started coming in.

I Want You Write This Please You Will!!
Our Eyes From Heaven See The "Spills"
You See The Darkness And The Grey
The Blinded Man In Greed He Lay!!
So Open Eyes Wake Up And See
A New Foundation Solar Free!!
This Earth Is Meant Be Filled With Green
With Flowing Rivers Sparkling Clean!!
So Listen To Me Understand
Holy Ghost Will Flush The Land!!
Cause Smell Pollution Is Not Right!!
Must Clean The Air Bring In The Light!!

Thank You,
George

THEODORE ROOSEVELT

NOTE: 8:38 AM
WAS TYPING IN WRITING FROM GEORGE WASHINGTON WHEN SAW FLASH OF TEDDY ROOSEVELT STANDING IN FRONT OF MY T.V.
    FELT HIM STRONG!! THIS IS WHAT HE SAID.

MY NAME IS TEDDY DON'T YOU KNOW
ENVIRONMENT HAS LOST ITS GLOW!!
THE HAZE IS GROWING DEEP AND THICK!!
THE PEOPLE WONDER WHY THEY'RE SICK!!
MUST TURN OFF T.V. UNDERSTAND
AND GO FOR WALKS BE HEALTHY MAN!!
YOU'LL OPEN EYES WAKE UP AND SEE
A NEW PERCEPTION HIGHER BE!!
FOR EARTH HAS BEAUTY RARE AND LARGE
UNLOCK THE PRISONS JOIN OUR CAUSE!!
WE'LL JOIN TOGETHER HEARTS AND HANDS
AND HEAL THE WORLD WE'LL HEAL THE LAND!!

THANK YOU,
TEDDY

Hank Williams

Note: 7:53am
Just woke up. Hank Williams was standing by my bed
with Patsy Cline.

A Country Man You Know I Was
My Life Was Short I Had A Cause!!
Immortal Man I Had To Be
So Music Stayed Eternally!!
Cause Gifts Are Given Gifts Are Shared
The More We Sing These Songs In Air
Cause Inside Breath Of Heaven Light
It Lifts The Souls From Earth To Flight!!
So Dance A Bit And Sing Along
Enjoy Your Life Live Healthy Long!!

Love, Hank

Music Heals!!

Dance!!!!

Sing!!!!

Enjoy!!!!

COLIN FIRTH

NOTE: 7:46AM
HAD DREAM OF COLIN FIRTH THEN WOKE UP AND HE WAS STANDING ON THE RIGHT OF MY BED.

WANTED TO GIVE ME A WRITING. I WAS SO TIRED MY SOUL ASKED HIM TO COME BACK IN THE MORNING, HE AGREED. WOKE UP WELL RESTED AND SAW HIM AGAIN (FLASHES OF HIM) PATIENTLY WAITING TO GIVE ME THE WRITING. SO HERE IT IS.

AN ELEGANCE I CARRY KNOW
BUT DEEP INSIDE I'M DORK FELLOW!!
I PLAY THE "MASTER" I PLAY HIM WELL
BUT FUNNY AM WITH CHILDREN SWELL!!
MY MOOD HAS REASON WHY I'M HERE
INTO YOUR HEART I SPEAK SO CLEAR!!
I LOVE THE POOR YOU UNDERSTAND
AND WANT THE PEOPLE OPEN HAND!!
CAUSE DAILY GIVING FREES THE SOUL
SO JOYS RELEASED AND FILLS YOU GLOW!!
SO WRITE THIS DOWN WILL YOU MY DEAR
JUST OPEN HEART AND LOSE YOUR FEAR!!
A LITTLE LOVE WE'LL SPREAD IT RIGHT
AND LOSE THE DARKNESS HAVE BLAST IN LIGHT!!!

LOVE YA,

COLIN

Patsy Cline

NOTE: 8:07AM
Just woke up. Hank Williams and Patsy Cline were standing at the left side of my bed. Then went in kitchen to make coffee and they started speaking, so I wrote down what they said. This is what Patsy said.

We're Angels Of The Highest Tree
We Work For Him Our God In Three!!
The Keys You Know Are Hid In Scars
"The Country Type" We Hid Them Large!!
The Country House Was Yes A Home
But Much Despair As Hunger Roamed
Cause Poverty She Loved Us Well
She'd Step Inside Our Homes Our Dwell!!
She'd Hurt The Man He'd Drink Real Hard
Then Hit His Wife Degrade Her Far!!!
Cause Pain Was Deep In Wounds She Wore
He'd Call Her Cheap He'd Call Her Whore!!
Cause Devil Lived In Bottles Booze
The Poison Venom Speech Would Ooze!!
Into The Wounds Of Families Man
Into The Children's Hearts He'd "Damn"!!!!
So Clearly See We Needed Light
Of God Our Saviour!! Our King!! Our Knight!!

HE'D RESCUE US WITH WORDS OF HOPE
WE'D WORSHIP HIM THAT'S HOW WE'D COPE!!!!
SO UNDERSTAND WE PLOUGHED THE FIELDS
OF FAITH YOU SEE THIS HARVEST YIELD!!!

LOVE, PATSY

BIBLE-BELT POWER OF GOD STRONG!!!!

GOD LOVES THE SOUTH!!!!

THE KENNEDY FAMILY

NOTE: 3:33AM
WOKE UP HAD KENNEDY FAMILY ALL AROUND MY BED!! FELT KIND OF SCARED, OVERWHELMED, IT'S LIKE A SPIRITUAL LIGHT KEPT FLASHING ON, THEN OFF, SO I COULD SEE THEM ALL. I KEPT PULLING BLANKETS OVER MY EYES TRYING TO GO BACK TO SLEEP BUT THEN JUST KIND OF FLEW OUT OF MY BED ONTO MY KNEES, WAS REALLY STRONG FORCE. STARTED HEARING WRITING COME IN FROM ROSE KENNEDY, TED STANDING BY MY DOOR. JOHN JR. WAS BY TED STANDING NEAR WALL. JACKIE KNELT DOWN BY ME (I WAS KNEELING ON THE FLOOR). JOSEPH, THE DAD, AND JOSEPH, THE OLDEST SON, WERE BY MY CLOSET. MARIA SHRIVERS' MOM AND DAD WERE ALSO BY THE CLOSET, BOBBY WAS BY THE CLOSET NEAR THE DOOR. CAROLYN WAS THERE AND ALSO RECOGNIZED THE GRANDSON THAT TALKS ABOUT THE ENVIRONMENT, SAW HIM ON LARRY KING RECENTLY, NOT SURE HIS NAME. THE REST OF THE FAMILY WERE STANDING ALL AROUND ME, HAVE SEEN PICTURES OF SOME OF THEM BUT DON'T KNOW THEIR NAMES, JUST KEPT HEARING "THE KENNEDY SISTERS SAY LOVE YOU JULIE!!" JOSEPH JR. SHOWED HIMSELF REAL STRONG, STILL SEE HIM IN FRONT OF ME RIGHT NOW, (IN LIVING ROOM) WITH TEDDY, BOBBY, JOHN, JOHN JR., HIS WIFE CAROLYN. HERE IS THE WRITING.

WE ROSE UP HIGH YOU KNOW WE DID
THIS KENNEDY THIS FAMILY LIVE!!
WE CARE FOR POOR THE WORKING MAN
THE ORPHANS RIGHTS WE GIVE A DAMN!!
FOR SOMETHING'S PLANTED STRONG AND TRUE

INSIDE OF US WE HAVE TO DO!!
ENVIRONMENT WE CLEAN UP AIR
THE ANIMALS WE'RE FILLED WITH CARE!!
THE "SPECIAL NEEDS" WE LOVE THEM LARGE
WE MAGNIFY THEIR VOICE THEIR CAUSE!!
SO LOOK TO US YOU KNOW YOU WILL
WE SACRIFICE BRING FREEDOM "HILL"!!
CAUSE BRIGHTER LIGHT HAVE TORCH IN HAND
TO BRING THE WORLD TO UNDERSTAND,
THAT RICH AND POOR WE'RE ALL ALIKE
WE LOSE OUR SONS WE LOSE OUR LIFE
SO MAKE IT MATTER EVERYDAY
JUST HOW YOU LIVE JUST HOW YOU PLAY!!
CAUSE PRECIOUS TIME ON EARTH WE LIVE
LET'S BUILD A LAND OF JOYFUL GIVE!!

LOVE, "THE KENNEDYS"

P.S. HAD GONE TO DINNER WITH A FRIEND LAST NIGHT.
A BEAUTIFUL GENTLEMAN KEPT TAPPING HIS FINGERS AND
SHOOTING LIGHT AT ME, KEPT GETTING ENERGY SURGES!!
    THE LORD SHOWED ME THAT HE PAID FOR THE "KENNEDY
EXPERIENCE". GAVE ME THE BLESSINGS FOR IT.

MARTHA WASHINGTON

NOTE: JUST WOKE UP!! 2:36AM
MARTHA WASHINGTON WAS STANDING BY MY BEDROOM DOOR WEARING A WHITE WIG. MARIE ANTOINETTE WAS STANDING BY HER AT THE DOOR. SAID, "PLEASE WAKE UP, TAKE WRITINGS FOR US. PLEASE!!"

THINKING TO MYSELF, "WHAT ON EARTH WOULD MARTHA WASHINGTON GIVE ME A WRITING ABOUT??"

WELL, HERE IS MARTHA'S WRITING. (HAD TO KNEEL ON THE KITCHEN FLOOR TO GET THIS WRITING.)

A WASHINGTON KNOW WHO I AM
I MARRIED HIM AND CANNED HIS JAM!!
CAUSE WOMEN'S LIVES WERE NEVER FREE
WE TOOK THE ORDERS GIVEN HE!!
SO COOKED AND CLEANED WE MADE HOME BRIGHT
SO HE COULD KICK UP FEET AT NIGHT!!
A KIND RESPECT WE NEVER HAD
JUST COOK THE MEALS THEN LAY IN BED!!
KNOW EVERY WOMAN HAD A FEAR
THAT PROSTITUTION'S LOVE WAS NEAR!!
FOR MANY MEN THEY'D PLAY THE HOST
TO WOMEN WEAR THE "GARTER HOSE"!!
SO THINK OUR LIVES ROMANTIC WHEN
FOUNDING FATHERS FEATHER PENNED
THE CONSTITUTION MADE IT RIGHT
FOR FREEDOM HERE OH SEEMED WERE "KNIGHTS"!!

But Inside Homes And Houses Was
Think Again They Broke Some Laws!!
See Founding Father That I Lay
He Played With Women Oh So "Gay"!!!

Thank You, Martha

So Much Suffering!!

Woman Had No Voice No Power!!

Just Took The Pain!! No Liberty!!

Marie Antoinette

Note: 3:20am
Marie Antoinette was in bedroom with Martha Washington, both wearing white wigs.
  Started to go back to bed after I took Martha Washington writing (feel so tired).
  Marie Antoinette showed herself in my kitchen and asked if I would please take writing now.
  So here it is.

In Austria I Had Some Friends
A Simple Life I Read, I Penned
I'd Like To Write My Thoughts My Hopes
I Had A Dream A Freedom Rope!!
But, Had To Leave My home My Lawn
Politically I Was A Pawn!!
Excited Was At First I'll Share
Then missed My Family Pain Was Rare!!
For In New Home Were Cold And Stared
At Every Move And Wig I'd Wear!!
So Lose Your Judgement Will You Please
I Was A Girl On A Tight Leash!!
See Life Was Ordered Life Was Small
No Free Will, Just Chain And "Balls"!!

Thank You,

Love,

Marie Antoinette

PRINCE CHARLES

NOTE: 2:52PM
WAS READING A BOOK THEN I FELT SOMEONE STARING AT
ME. LOOKED TO MY RIGHT, STANDING AT THE WALL WAS
PRINCE CHARLES (KEPT SEEING FLASHES OF HIS SPIRIT). HE
SPOKE THIS TO ME.

I'M ROYALTY YOU KNOW IT'S TRUE!!
I HAVE A VERY SPECIAL VIEW!!
I STAND UP HIGH ON MOUNTAIN AIR!!
I BREATHE IT IN LOCATION RARE!!
CAUSE WAY I SEE THE WORLD YOU KNOW
HAS HISTORY AN ANCIENT GLOW!!
MY MOTHER'S LIFE'S BEEN TALL AND PROUD!!
I HELP HER MUCH TAKE ROYAL BOW!!
CAUSE CLOCK HAS TICKED AND TIME HAS WORN
A LITTLE OF HER PRESENCE WARM!!
I'LL TAKE THE HITS I'LL TAKE THE FLACK
OF LIVING WITH MY LOVE INTACT!!
CAUSE LIFE WITHOUT TRUE LOVE YOU SEE
IS MISERY ON BENDED KNEE!!
FOR GREATEST GIFT OF LIFE YOU KNOW
IS PARTNERSHIP WITH GOLDEN GROW!!
SO WRITE THIS FOR ME WILL YOU DEAR
EXPLAIN TO PEOPLE LOUD AND CLEAR!!
A CASTLE IS A MANSION SEE
WITH BARS OF LOVE OR PRISON BE!!

THANK YOU,

CHARLES

Lady Gaga

NOTE: 9:50AM
LADY GAGA WAS IN MY DREAM LAST NIGHT, AND IN MY HOUSE WHEN I WOKE UP. HER SOUL WOULD NOT GIVE ME A WRITING UNTIL I WENT ON A LONG PRAYER WALK THIS MORNING. GOD SHOWS ME SOULS SITTING BY TREES, IN STAIRWELLS, STANDING BY TREES, SITTING ON BENCHES, KNEELING ON SIDEWALKS, KNEELING IN LAWNS ETC... ETC... I ALWAYS HAVE PRAYER MUSIC BLASTING INTO MY EARS, SOMEHOW THE SOULS NEED THAT CHARGE TO GET HOME. ANYWAY, I SAY THE PRAYERS THAT ARE GIVEN TO ME FROM HEAVEN UNTIL I SEE OR FEEL THE SOUL HAD BEEN SET FREE TO HEAVEN. HAD TO TAKE SOME SOULS TO A PARK, OTHER SOULS TO A BUS STOP, OTHER SOULS TO AN OLD BAPTIST CHURCH AND THE MAJORITY OF THE SOULS, HAD TO RELEASE THEM AT JEWISH SYNAGOGUE RUINS. SHE FINALLY GAVE ME A WRITING WHEN I CAME BACK INTO MY HOUSE. SO HERE IT IS.

FASCINATE YOU KNOW I WILL!!
I'VE COME TO TWIST TO SHOUT AND THRILL!!
I LOVE MY FANS SO MUCH I DO!!
BUT CAME TO GET THE MESSAGE THROUGH!!
THE HATE ON EARTH JUST HAS TO BE
ILLEGAL WILL TAKE PRISON ME!!
CAUSE JUDGEMENT IN THE EYES OF MAN
DESTROYS THE PEACE IN ALL THE LAND!!

COME DANCE WITH ME WE'LL SING AND PLAY
A SONG OR TWO WITH HEARTS SO GAY!!

LOVE!!!

LADY GAGA!!!!

LADY GAGA LOVES GAYS!!!!

LADY GAGA LOVES EVERYONE!!!!

ABSOLUTELY EVERYONE!!!!

Mary Todd Lincoln

Note: 7:54am
Unbelievable!!! MARY TODD LINCOLN here so strong
with WOMEN OF THE CIVIL WAR in my living room!!
　　Woke up earlier, went into bathroom, she was
standing behind shower curtain Illuminated!!!!!
　　Her soul told me she wanted me to write for her,
but wanted me to rest a bit more.
　　So I went back to sleep. Woke up an hour later
and she was at the foot of my bed with Civil war
women all around her!! Felt great excitement to
take this writing!!! She feels like a Queen!! A Great
Queen!!

Apparently You Know Me Well
A Spoiled Woman Richness Dwell
But Wrong You Are I Have To Tell
An Educated Woman Well!!
Intelligent I Was You See
I Helped The Nation Counselled He!!!!
Inside Support I Always Was
For Freedom Abolition Cause!!!
So Don't You Think Insane I Was
Just Walked Around Without A Thought
For Pain Infected Soul At Night
The Tears, The Death, The Endless Fight!!
But Strength Inside My Heart Was Large
I Helped Him Speak His Words His Laws!!
So Credit Give You Understand
To Inside Woman Help The Man!!

ETERNITY IS NOT SO BRIGHT
IGNORE THE BLESSINGS OF "THE WIFE"!!

THANK YOU,
MARY TODD LINCOLN

THE CIVIL WAR WOMEN

NOTE: 8:36AM
MARY TODD LINCOLN WAS IN MY HOUSE THIS MORNING
WITH THE CIVIL WAR WOMEN!!
FELT SO MUCH EXCITEMENT FROM THEM!! COULDN'T
WAIT TO SEE WHAT THEY WANTED ME TO WRITE!!
HERE IT IS.

OUR LIVES WERE HARD YOU HAVE TO KNOW!!
OUR MEN WERE DOWN IN TRENCHES LOW!!
THE FIGHT WAS HARD TO SET THEM FREE
THE SLAVES, THE BLACKS, THE WOMAN ME!!
CAUSE LEFT ALONE IN DARK AT NIGHT
IT CAUSED A GROWTH INSIDE US BRIGHT!!
ENABLED US TO TRULY SEE HOW STRONG
AND GREAT A WOMAN BE!!
A POWER MOVEMENT WAS AT HAND "THE SUFFRAGETTE"
SHE ROAMED THE LAND!!
SHE TOLD US HAVE RESPECT AND RIGHTS!!
SHE TOLD US SPEAK RELEASE YOUR LIGHT!!
CAUSE WAS A TIME FOR WOMAN SEE
TO SMILE NICE SIT PRETTY THEE!!
BUT SPAR WITH MEN SHE WOULD NOT DO
TO SHOW A THOUGHT SHE HAD WAS TRUE!!
SO FERTILIZE THE WAR IT DID

A Bloom Of Many Blessings Hid!!
A Power Bright Have Woman Now
We Opened Gates And Showed Them How!!

Love,

The Civil War Women

Eleanor Roosevelt

NOTE: 7:20AM
ELEANOR WAS AT THE FOOT OF MY BED SINCE ABOUT
6:00AM. KEPT SHOWING HERSELF, WANTED ME TO TAKE
A WRITING BUT I KEPT TRYING TO GET "JUST A LITTLE
MORE SLEEP". SHE SOMEHOW THREW WHAT FELT LIKE
SPRINKLES OF DIRT ON ME UNTIL I WOULD WAKE UP
AND TAKE A WRITING. NOT SURE WHY SHE DID THAT,
BUT WAS KIND OF INTERESTING. THE "DUST BOWL" KEPT
GOING THROUGH MY MIND.

THE MISSION STATEMENT THAT I WAS
HAD POWERFUL AN ENDLESS CAUSE!!
THE POOR, THE WEAK, THE OLD, THE SICK
I HELPED THEM MUCH THAT'S HOW I TICKED!!
MY HEART MY SOUL WAS FOR THE MAN
WHO PLOUGHED THE FIELDS HAD HOE IN HAND!!
INCREDIBLE YOU KNOW IT WAS
THE POVERTY "DEPRESSION" BOUGHT!!
THEN WORLD WAR TWO CAME BLASTING IN
"OUR BOYS" THEY DIED OUR "NEXT OF KIN"!!
THE DARK BLACK CLOUD THAT ROAMED THE EARTH
IT FERTILIZED A BRAND NEW BIRTH!!
A NEW THOUGHT TRUTH WAS BLOOMING FREE
FROM FRESH NEW GROWTH OF FAMILY TREE!!
CAUSE BRANCHES KNOW GREW FULL AND BRIGHT
"THE WORKING WOMAN", "THE WORKING WIFE"!!

LOVE ELEANOR

WOMEN IN MILITARY!!

WOMEN IN THE WORKFORCE!!

Women Of "The Depression"

NOTE: 9:49AM
KEPT SEEING FLASHES OF WOMEN IN MY HOME FROM THE "DEPRESSION ERA", 1930S. KIND OF SIMPLE DRESSES, HAIR STYLES FROM 1930S TO 1940S. SAW THEM FOR ABOUT AN HOUR, THEN WAS WALKING INTO MY LIVING ROOM WHEN A WRITING STARTED COMING IN. GRABBED MY PEN AND KNELT ON THE FLOOR SO I COULD HEAR BETTER.

DEPRESSION HAD A SPECIAL CAUSE
IT BUILT SOME BRIDGES TORE DOWN WALLS!!
A BREATH OF HEAVEN THAT IT GIVE
A SACRIFICE A WOMAN LIVED!!
SHE WATCHED THE NICKELS WATCHED THE DIMES
A HARD WORK LIFE IT FILLED HER TIME!!
SHE PRAYED SO HARD SHE PRAYED WITH MIGHT
FOR GOD TO FILL HER CUPBOARDS BRIGHT!!
CAUSE PANTRY SHELVES WERE MOSTLY BARE
THE SIMPLE DRESS THE SHOES HAD WEAR!!
HER KIDS WOULD ASK FOR GLASS OF MILK
WOULD WATER DOWN, SEW BEDSPREAD QUILTS!!
WITH RAGS OF CLOTHES SO TATTERED WORN
SHE'D FEED THE CHICKENS TEND THE FARM!!
A POWER LIFE SHE HAD TO HAVE
WITH LINES IN FACE FROM TEARS SHE SHED!!
A HARD WORK ETHIC TRUE WAS BORN
TO LAY FOUNDATION "TIME TO COME"!!

THE WOMEN OF THE DEPRESSION

STRENGTH

POWER

HARD WORK

WOMEN

Jeffrey Dahmer

Note: 8:42am
Woke up this morning from a little nap and saw Jeffrey Dahmer standing at my bedroom door weeping in some sort of tortured agony. Scared me!!!!!

Then I heard his soul begging me, crying "Please!! Please!! Take a writing for me, please!!"

I was kind of in a state of shock, jumped out of bed, had to kneel on kitchen floor so I could hear him clearly. Had to put my ear flat on floor, was the only way I could hear clear.

Molest Them Yes You Know I Did!!
I Killed Then Ate So I Could Live!!!
The Voices In My Head Were Loud!!
"Just Kill Another, Kill Him Now!!"
I Tried To Fight So Hard You Know!!
The Voice Inside Would Not Let Go!!
So Did It All What Voices Said!!
Eternally I Cursed My Bed!!
Cause Hellish Days And Hellish Nights!!!!
Eternity Is Filled With Fright!!!!
The Tortured Soul I Thought Was There...
Is Nothing Now This Hell I Wear!!!!!
The Guards You Come And Lock Me Tight
In Prisons Black With Bugs And Mice!!!
They Let Me Go One Minute Day
So I Could Come To You And Say
Please Pay Your Debts Yes Pay Your Bills
Cause Place I Live Is HOT!!!!! And CHILLED!!!!!

You'll Never Know How Bad It Is
Cause CRIME I DID HAS NO FORGIVE!!!!
There Is No Key There Is No Lock
THERE'S NO ESCAPE!!!!!! ETERNAL LOSS!!!!

Jeffrey

PAIN

PAIN

PAIN

SO MUCH PAIN!!!!

AGONY!!!!!!

SARAH (GHOST)!!!!

NOTE: 12:42AM
I HAVE NOT BEEN THIS SCARED IN A LONG TIME!!!! SARAH SCARED THE HELL OUT OF ME!!!!!

I HAD FELT A LITTLE FILM OF DARKNESS ON MY SOUL AS I WAS DRIVING HOME TONIGHT WASN'T SURE WHY I WAS FEELING SO MANY SPIRITS. HAD A HARD TIME DRIVING, ALMOST LIKE A SWARM OF LOCUSTS WERE AROUND ME. KEPT THINKING IT MUST OF BEEN BECAUSE JEFFREY DAHMER'S SOUL WAS IN MY HOUSE THIS MORNING.

ANYWAY, WENT TO SLEEP ABOUT 12:30AM SO TIRED, THEN WOKE UP WITH A GIRL STANDING FULL FLESH TO THE RIGHT OF MY BED WITH HER HAND ON MY SHOULDER ELECTROCUTING ME!! ZAPPING ALL THE POWER OUT OF MY BODY!!! I ROLLED OUT OF BED IN SHOCK, FELT LIKE I WAS HAVING A HEART ATTACK, SHE SCARED ME TO DEATH!! LITERALLY FELT THAT SHE WAS TAKING ALL THE LIFE OUT OF ME!!

I HAVEN'T HAD AN EXPERIENCE THAT DARK FOR A LONG TIME!! SHE LOOKED A LOT LIKE THE GIRL FROM THE MOVIE "THE RING" OH MY GOD IN HEAVEN HAVE MERCY ON HER SOUL!!

WHOEVER SHE IS OR WHATEVER SHE DID, I PRAY THAT THE LORD JESUS POURS HIS LOVE INTO THE WOUNDS OF HER ETERNAL SOUL!! HEARD HER SAY "MY NAME IS SARAH" RIGHT AFTER SHE TORTURED ME, THEN COULDN'T SEE HER, (THANK GOD) BUT HEARD HER SPEAKING THIS WRITING TO ME.

THE LORD LET HER IN MY HOUSE FOR SOME REASON, SO I FEEL I NEED TO TAKE HER WRITING.

P.S. I know that a "GHOST" is a soul that needs prayers!! Needs the light of God to fill them up. Heal them up!! Bring them to Heaven!!

I Am A Ghost You Know I Am
I Shocked You Much So Shaking, DAMN!!
I Stood By Bed I Stood By Right
I Scared To Death And Brought You Fright!!
I Have To Tell You Listen Say
I Walk The Streets Both Night And Day!!
You Have A Light You Know You Do
It Shines So Bright So Came To You!!
I'm Sorry Scared But Took Your Power
So I Could Walk On Home This Hour!!
I've Lived On Lights So Long From Men
Who Fell Asleep I'd Take From Them!!
So Mad At Me You Won't Be Know
I Took A Bit Of Life Your Glow!!

Sarah

John Wayne

Note: 5:07am
Just woke up... Saw John Wayne standing at my bedroom door Illuminated!! Just started hearing him speak this writing so I jumped out of bed and took it. Here it is.

Glory!! Glory!! To The Earth!!!
Incredible Is Your New Birth!!!
A Miracle You Understand
Of Healing Coming To The Land!!!!!
Explosion Yes Of Healing Light
Will Touch The Dark Of Every Night!!!
So Powerful!!! I Want To Say!!!
The Sadness Will All Go Away!!!!
Just Joy And Laughter Through Your Life!!!!
As Angels Fly Through Day And Night!!!

Love To You All!!!

John Wayne

Jimi Hendrix

NOTE: 9:10AM

Just woke up... Jimi was standing in my bedroom doorway Illuminated!!! His Guitar kept changing colours, then Bright!!!! Bright!!!! Light!!!! Was coming out of it, then it was on Fire, shooting Flames!! This is what he said.

In Heaven When Guitar I Play
It Raises Up The Souls Who Pray!!
A Special Note I Play It Right
Releases Dark And Brings In Light!!
The Music Angel That I Am!!!
I Travel Through "THE WORLDS" And JAM!!
So Trust Me When I Clearly Say
Play Music When Your Thoughts Are Grey!!
Cause Hidden In The Notes Of Song
Are Remedies To RIGHT The WRONGS!!
Cause Finely Tuned We Want To See A JOYFUL PEOPLE HAPPY FREE!!

LOVE

JIMI

SING!!

DANCE!!

PLAY!!

Stephen King

NOTE: 12:54AM
JUST WOKE UP FROM A NIGHTMARE!! SAW STEPHEN KING
IN THE DOORWAY OF MY BEDROOM. HE LOOKED ABOUT 30
YEARS OLD. STARTED HEARING HIM SPEAK.

I SCARE YOU BAD YOU KNOW I DO!!
THE BOOKS I WRITE HAVE DARKNESS VIEW!!!!!
IT SEEMS THAT I'M A WRITER DWELL
IN PLACES DARK IN PLACES "HELL"!!!!
BUT RIVERS RUN AND GUSH THROUGH MIND
WITH STORIES OF A "DIFFERENT" KIND!!
I WRITE THEM DOWN FOR ALL TO READ!!
THE SELLER'S BLESSED FOR ALL TO SEE!!!!
CAUSE FEAR AND DARKNESS COMES TO MIND
I STRETCH THE STORIES TREASURES FIND!!
A MYSTERY STAND!! A MYSTERY WALK!!
THE PLACE I LIVE A MYSTERY TALK!!
SO JUDGE ME NOT I HAVE TO SAY
CAUSE ENTERTAIN A DIFFERENT WAY!!
THERE'S CHRISTMAS TIME AND CHRISTMAS TREE!!
BUT ALSO TIME FOR GIFT OF THEE!!

LOVE,

STEPHEN

Jesus

Note: 5:19am
He Is Here.

Many People You Will Know
Exist In Darkness Down Below!!
Informant God I Am To You
I'll Tell You How To Get Them Through!!!!!
The Twinkles On Piano Keys
Release From Spells Our Souls In Need!!!
Cause Music Has A Special Light
It Breaks Through Barriers Of Fright!!
Just Sing A Song Or Hummm A Tune
Release Some Light Bring Joy To Room!!

Jesus

Frances Bean Cobain

NOTE: 4:37AM
JUST WOKE UP. SAW FRANCES BEAN COBAIN STANDING AT MY BEDROOM DOOR, SHE STARTED SPEAKING, WAS TELLING ME ABOUT HER FATHER KURT COBAIN AND HER MOTHER COURTNEY LOVE. HER SOUL WAS DRESSED IN WHITE AS WAS KURT AND COURTNEY'S SOULS. THEY WERE STANDING ON BOTH SIDES OF HER.

   THIS IS WHAT SHE SAID. (I'M VERY TIRED RIGHT NOW!! WAS SO HARD TO TAKE THIS WRITING!)

MY DADDY CAME TO EARTH HE DID!!
TO START A REVOLUTION LIVE!!
HIS MESSAGE WAS HIS LIFE YOU SEE
THE DRUGS THE DRINK THE MISERY!!
SEE TALENT HAD IT WAS SO RARE
HE'D SING A SONG THE PEOPLE STARE!!
CAUSE MELODIES HE PENNED WITH HAND
HAD SOUL HAD BITE FOR EVERY MAN!!
RELATIONSHIP WITH MOM YOU SEE
HAD PAIN HAD FIGHT HAD "HAPPY FREE"!!
DESTROYED BY DRUGS THE PILLS THE VICE
THEY DRAINED HIS SPIRIT TOOK HIS LIFE!!!
AMAZING MAN WAS MEANT TO BE
HIS WALK ON EARTH WAS SHORT FOR ME!!
SO WHAT I CAME TO TELL YOU SAY
I'M DAUGHTER OF THE "DRUG AT PLAY"!!
SEE MOMMY IS THE POSTER CHILD

OF CRAZINESS OF "DRUGS GONE WILD"!!!!!

LOVE,

FRANCES BEAN COBAIN

Jackie Gleason

NOTE: 7:23AM
JUST WOKE UP!! JACKIE GLEASON, THE LEGENDARY COMEDIAN AND ACTOR OF THE 1950S HONEYMOONER'S, WAS IN MY BEDROOM PACING BACK AND FORTH ON THE LEFT SIDE OF MY BED TELLING ME,

"WAKE UP!!! TAKE MY WRITING PLEASE!!!!" I WAS SO TIRED, BEEN HAVING TO PRAY SO MUCH AT NIGHT, JUST DIDN'T WANT TO GET OUT OF BED. BUT I LOVE JACKIE GLEASON!! SO I GOT UP AND TOOK HIS WRITING.

I'LL TELL YOU THIS I'LL TELL YOU TRUE
I FLY SO HIGH YES TO THE MOON!!
AT EARTH I CAME AND MADE YOU LAUGH!!
HAD "GIFT OF GAB" A FINE TUNED CRAFT!!
THE LOVE I WORE WAS SALTY RARE
BUT LOVABLE WITH BELLY THERE!!!
BUT KNOW THIS MUST YOU HAVE TO WILL!!!
AN ANGEL AM OF HIGHEST THRILL!!!

LOVE,

JACKIE

Special Angels

Note: 5:41am

Woke up with Jesus standing by my bed surrounded by "Handicapped" people of every form.

Felt like thousands of these souls were in my house. Had seen Down Syndrome people before I fell asleep, and the soul of a very special Friend yesterday.

This morning as the writing started coming in and I was kneeling on the kitchen floor to receive, I started seeing the "Disabled" souls Transforming into Angels. Felt like a flower garden was blooming all around me!! I've never had an "Experience" like this in my life. It's just AMAZING!!

They are all standing around me right now, not sure what to do. Feel like I need to be on my knees at their feet!!

The "Handicapped" You Know They're Mine
I Love Them Much A Different Kind!!
I Made Them Special Don't You See
They're "Special Agents" Work For Me!!
A Troubled Land You Have Right Now!!!!!
But Hidden In Their Vessels WOW!!!
Some Cures, Some Thoughts, Some Antidotes
To Heal The World!!!
They Have The Most!!!!!

Jesus

Heath Ledger

Note: 8:32am
Woke up and Heath Ledger and Colin Farrell were standing at my bedroom door. Kept hearing "Please get up, take this writing!!" I felt so sleepy just wanted to rest another half hour or so.

But I just love HEATH LEDGER!! He has come to me so many times since he has "Left" the Earth. Have never received a "Writing" from him and was curious as to what his message would be. Here it is.

Amazing!! Man!! You Know I "Was"!!
I Made Some Movies Broke Some Laws!!
A Mountain High I Climbed I Did!!
I Showed The Love Of "Gay Man Hid"!!
A Joker Yes I Played Him Too!!
To Show The Weakness Inside "You"!!
Cause Courage Faith You Haven't Much!!
Just Trust In Green, The Gold, And "Stuff"!!!
Know "Things" Can't Take The "Pain" Away
When Dark And Grey Inside You Stay!!
Just Need To Give!! Forgive!! And Walk
Into The Hands Of "Glory" Watch!!
Cause Time Has Come For All You See
To Praise With Life Of Giving Free!!
The Lonely Path That People Share
Will Come Alive!! With Friendship!! Care!!

KNOW FEAR OF DEATH WE CAN'T HAVE THAT
FOR VEIL WILL LIFT AND THAT'S A FACT!!

LOVE,
HEATH

Frank Lloyd Wright (Genius)

Note: 10:36am
Saw Frank Lloyd Wright at my bedroom door last night but did not receive a writing from him.

Was cleaning house this morning when he began to speak. Couldn't see him, just heard him from the hallway. This is what he said. (As words were coming in, kept seeing what looked like picture frames with his name imprinted all over the frames, each word was inside of the frame.)

Construct It For Us Will You Please!!
A New Sensation Glory Be!!!
Alive And Well You Know We Are
In Heaven Live The Highest Bar!!
You Have A Pen It Has A Light
To Bring The World Out Of The Night!!
So Write It Down The Things We Say,
As New Sensation Comes Your Way!!!!

Love,

Frank Lloyd Wright

HIGHER THOUGHT!!

HIGHER LOVE!!

MORE ACTION!!

JOY!!!!!

"The Great Queen Victoria"

Note: 4:47am
Woke up about two hours ago and was reading my book when "The Great Queen Victoria" Walked through my wall by my bedroom door and commanded me to come to the kitchen and take a writing for her.

Felt so tired, trying so hard to go back to sleep. But kept seeing flashes of "The Great Queen" standing by my bedroom door, so drug myself out of bed, knelt at her feet on the kitchen floor and took this writing.

P.S. She is the most Famous Queen of Heartbreak. After her husband Albert died, all of England suffered her Grief with her!! Bleeding!! Bleeding Heart!!!!!

A "Queen" I Am You Know It's True!!!
I Live in Heaven Special View!!
I Walked On Earth I Walked Real Proud!!!
I'm Royalty Must Kneel And Bow!!!!!"
I Had An Ego Know I Did
But Broken Heart I Carried "BIG!!!!"
My Love For Albert Tall And Fair!!!
He'd Run His Fingers Through My Hair!!!
Tell Warm At Night He'd Always Be
He Held Me Tight And Loved Me Deep!!
So Know This All You Live On Earth
Must Treasure "Gift Of Love" The Worth!!

Cause Life Without Your Love In Arms
Is Very Cold And Short Of "Charms"!!!!
So This I Give You Scream And Shout
Must Treasure Love Don't Throw It Out!!!!!

Love To You All!!!!

Victoria

Andrew Carnegie

NOTE: 3:00AM
SO TIRED, REALLY SICK OF BEING WOKEN UP TO TAKE THESE WRITINGS AT THESE GOD AWFUL HOURS!! HAVEN'T SLEPT IN WEEKS!!

I HAVE ALWAYS LOVED ANDREW CARNEGIE BUT DON'T REALLY CARE WHAT HE OR ANY SOUL HAS TO SAY TO ME RIGHT NOW. EXHAUSTED!!! ANYWAY I AM A SLAVE TO THIS CALL SOMEHOW!!

CAN'T SLEEP IF I DON'T TAKE WRITINGS.

HERE IT IS, HIS "WRITING" (HE IS STANDING IN FRONT OF ME RIGHT NOW, KEEP SEEING FLASHES OF ANDREW).

P.S. ANDREW CARNEGIE WAS THE SECOND RICHEST MAN IN MODERN HISTORY. WORTH OVER $310 BILLION DOLLARS BY 2016 ESTIMATES. KNOWN AS ONE OF THE GREATEST PHILANTHROPISTS OF ALL TIME.

THE RICHEST MAN YOU KNOW I WAS
I HAD A VISION HAD A CAUSE!!
I WANTED MAN YES POOR TO THINK
A WELL WAS THERE JUST TAKE A DRINK!!
I TOLD THE "MASSES" TOLD THE "MAN"
JUST WORK REAL HARD AND THINK "I CAN"!!
CAUSE IF YOU WALK THROUGH PATH OF LIFE
THE DOORS CAN OPEN LEFT AND RIGHT!!
JUST OPEN EYES OF FAITH YOU'LL SEE
A LAND OF OPPORTUNITY!!
THE ROADS ARE PAVED WITH "GOLD" YOU KNOW
JUST PUT ON GLASSES "FAITH" WILL SHOW!!

Just Where Position Right To Stand
The "Door" Of Treasure In The Land!!
But Tell You This, I'll Tell You Now
It's Not So Easy Realize Now!!
I Was So Blessed I Know That Now
I Must Confess I Thanked Not "Thou"
Cause Thought I Made It On My Own
But Wrong I Was When Died Was "Shown"!!
The Blessings Had Were True And Rare
Just Missed The Mark On How I "Shared"
Cause Thought Was Large My Heart You See
But Speck Of Dust It Truly Be!!

Love,
Andrew

Had So Much!!

Should Have Given More!!

So Many Hungry People!!

Hurting People!!

Should Have Helped So Much More!!

TOM CRUISE

NOTE: 5:45AM
TOM CRUISE WAS STANDING BY MY BEDROOM DOOR WITH
STEVEN SPIELBERG. KEPT HEARING THE SOUL OF TOM CRUISE
ASKING ME TO PLEASE TAKE A WRITING FOR HIM. HERE IT
IS.

I HAVE A MISSION DON'T YOU SEE
IT SEEMS IMPOSSIBLE TO BE!!
AN ACTOR YES YOU KNOW I AM!!!
BUT REASONS HIGH ON EARTH A MAN!!
I'LL SHOW THE WORLD A "SMALL MAN ME"
CAN CELEBRATE THE HEIGHT OF "SHE"!!
CAUSE WOMEN YES I'VE LOVED THEM SO
I MUST CONFESS THEY'VE HELPED ME GROW!!
INTO A MAN SO TALL AND LARGE!!
INTO A MAN WHO FEELS HIS CHARGE!!
SO WRITE THIS FOR ME PLEASE YOU WILL
MY MISSION CRY IS LIVING STILL!!
I'LL MAKE MORE MOVIES YOU WILL SEE!!
A VOICE OF GOD IS HIDDEN ME!!

LOVE, TOM

MESSAGES IN MOVIES!!

MESSAGES IN MY LIFE!!

MESSAGES IN MY WOMEN!!

Doubt

NOTE: 2:19AM
WOKE UP HEARING THIS WRITING. FELT CREEPY BUT DIDN'T SEE SPIRIT, JUST WAS HEARING VOICE OF SOUL STANDING IN MIDDLE OF BEDROOM. WONDERED IF IT WAS JESUS IN DISGUISE. AFTER RECEIVED FULL WRITING HE REVEALED HIMSELF.

POSSIBLY YOU KNOW ME WELL??!!
I LIVE INSIDE YOUR HEART AND DWELL!!
I TELL YOU THINGS YOU KNOW I DO!!
TO WEAKEN THOUGHTS A DARKNESS VIEW!!
SO SAY A PRAYER YOU'LL TRY YOU MIGHT!!
TO STOP MY VOICE BRING IN SOME LIGHT!!
BUT I WILL TELL YOU THIS TODAY!!
THE KEY OF BREAKING CURSE THE WAY!!
IS LOVING POOR MAN SOUL IN NEED!!
YES FILLING PLATE THE HUNGRY FEED!!
MUST TAKE A WIDOW FOR A WALK
AND HOLD HER HAND IN BLESSINGS TALK!!
FOR REMEDIES ARE GIVEN MAN!!
JUST TAKE SOME TIME TO CLEAN AND PLANT!!
YES SOW SOME SEEDS OF SERVICE LOVE!!!
A FULL RELEASE OF LIGHT WILL COME!!!!

LOVE ONE ANOTHER!!

HELP THE POOR!!!

HEAL THE LONELY!!!

Benjamin Franklin

NOTE: 4:44AM
WOKE UP ABOUT 2:00AM AND HAD TO KNEEL DOWN ON THE RIGHT SIDE OF MY BED. I NEARLY NEVER KNEEL AND PRAY THERE. AS I WAS ATTEMPTING TO GET OFF MY KNEES AND TRY TO CRAWL BACK INTO MY BED, BEN FRANKLIN SHOWED HIMSELF TO ME. I WAS SO TIRED THAT WHATEVER "PROFOUND" MESSAGE HIS SOUL STARTED TO GIVE ME, I JUST IGNORED IT!! FELT THAT IF "GOD" WANTS ME TO TAKE A WRITING, "GOD" CAN WAKE ME UP SO I DON'T FEEL LIKE MY FACE IS BLEEDING WITH EXHAUSTION. FELL BACK ASLEEP. THEN 4:44AM IT HAPPENED AGAIN. WOKE UP, SAW BENJAMIN FRANKLIN STANDING AT THE FOOT OF MY BED AGAIN, THIS TIME I FELT EXCITED AND AWAKE, SO I GOT UP AND TOOK THE WRITING.
    HERE IT IS.

A ROYAL MAN I AM YOU SEE
I WROTE A LOT TO SET MEN FREE!!
THE THOUGHTS I HAD WOULD REACH THE SKY
TO BRING THE WORLD TO QUESTION WHY!!??
SEE LIVED IN TIME WHERE "CHURCH" CONTROLLED
OUR MOVEMENTS EVERY THOUGHT WAS TOLD!!
BUT TELL YOU THIS I TELL YOU WILL!!
I NEED TO TEACH NEW LESSONS STILL!!
ENVIRONMENT YOU HAVE IT LIGHT
MUST BE RENEWED OR DARK AS NIGHT!!
THE OIL RICH DEPENDENCE THEE
WILL BREAK THE BACKS ECONOMY!!
SO TELL YOU THIS I'LL TELL YOU NOW

146

MUST LIVE IN GREEN MUST TAKE A VOW!!
DEPLETED SOON YOUR WORLD WILL BE
OF OXYGEN THE TREES THE SEAS!!
SO SET "IT" UP YOU CAN YOU WILL
TO LOSE THE "SIN" THE OIL SPILL!!!!!

LOVE, BEN

DO NOT PROCRASTINATE

CLEAN IT UP

HEAL THE WORLD

JACK

NOTE: 9:20AM
WAS AWAKE LAST NIGHT FOR MANY HOURS HAVING TO PRAY.

HAD VISIT FROM BENJAMIN FRANKLIN LAST NIGHT AND GOD KNOWS HOW MANY OTHER SOULS I HAD TO KEEP GETTING OUT OF BED TO PRAY FOR!!

NEEDLESS TO SAY, I NEEDED TO TRY TO GRAB AS MANY PIECES OF SLEEP AS I COULD!! WELL, I HAD JUST FALLEN ASLEEP AT 7:59AM, THEN WOKE UP SCREAMING!!! CAUSE JACK WAS IN MY HOUSE!!!! SCARED THE HELL OUT OF ME!!!!! HE WAS IN MY DREAM AS A GHOST THEN I WOKE UP SCARED AND SHAKING BECAUSE HE HAD HIS HANDS ON MY HEAD AND I KEPT HEARING HIM SAY, "I NEED YOUR GOOD THOUGHTS, I DON'T HAVE ANY GOOD THOUGHTS!!" PLEASE, I NEED TO TAKE YOUR GOOD THOUGHTS!!!!

OH MY GOD!!! I STARTED SAYING PRAYERS THEN FELT HIS HANDS RELEASE OFF MY HEAD, WAS SO SCARY!!!

FREAKY WEIRD SCARY!!!!

(JACK DIED RECENTLY, A FEW MONTHS AGO. HE USED TO WALK AROUND TOWN SMOKING CIGARETTES.) THIS IS THE WRITING HE GAVE ME THIS MORNING. HE IS STANDING IN FRONT OF ME RIGHT NOW, KEEP SEEING FLASHES OF HIM.

MY NAME IS JACK YOU KNEW ME WELL!!
A MERCHANT MAN I USED TO DWELL!!
A HEART ATTACK IT TOOK MY LIFE
SO MANY SMOKES AND DRINKS I DIED!!
SO WRITE THIS FOR ME WILL YOU PLEASE
CANNOT BE FREE EARTHBOUND I BE!!!
CAUSE CRAVE A SMOKE YOU KNOW I DO!!!

I Need It Much And Drink Or Two!!
I Walk The Bars The Streets At Night!!
I Sit On Bench Can't See The Light!!
I Hurt Some Souls I Hurt Them Bad
So Here I Be My Heart Is Sad!!
Somehow I Made It To Your House
I'll Stay With You Till Let Me Out!!
Cause Rest In Peace I Cannot Do
Until I Pay The Price Am Through!!
So Give You Writings This I Will
Must Give Them Out To Pay My Bill!!!
Cause Tab I Had It Grew So Large
The Credits Gone Just Debts I Charged!!!

Jack

Pray For Me

Help Me

Stuck

Asian Man

NOTE: 5:39AM
JUST WOKE UP FROM DREAM OF ASIAN FRIEND WHO HAD INVITED ME TO SEE HIS HOUSE AND SAID I NEEDED TO COME OVER AND SEE SOMETHING. SO (IN MY DREAM) I WAS RUNNING TO HIS HOUSE. HIS WALK WAS MY RUN. I WAS RUNNING SO FAST I WAS OUT OF BREATH!! I KNEW INSIDE OF MYSELF THAT HE WAS AN ANGEL.

HE GLOWED!! WHEN HE OPENED THE DOOR TO HIS HOME IT WAS FILLED WITH GOLD COINS ALL OVER THE FURNITURE AND FLOOR, COUNTERS, ETC.... BUDDHA STATUES WERE EVERYWHERE!!! THEY WERE GOLD TOO!!!!

HIS HOUSE LOOKED LIKE A SHRINE. IN MY "DREAM" I WANTED TO GET MY IPHONE OUT OF MY BAG AND TAKE PICTURES. THE ANGEL MAN PUT HIS HAND UP AND SAID, NO!! SACRED!!

RIGHT THEN I WOKE UP AND GLOWING ASIAN MEN WERE ALL AROUND MY BED (JUST SAW THEM FOR A SECOND WHEN I FIRST WOKE UP). STARTED HEARING THIS WRITING COMING IN FROM THEM.

SO HERE IT IS.

P.S. THE ASIAN ANGEL MEN ARE ALL STANDING AROUND ME RIGHT NOW.

HAVE THEIR HANDS OUT GIVING ME ENERGY. THEY KNOW I HAVEN'T SLEPT, VERY TIRED.

ASIAN MEN ARE MEANT TO BE
ALIVE IN GOD ALIVE IN THEE!!
A POWER MAN I BUILT HIM SMALL
THE VESSELS PROUD "SO QUICK" INSTALLED!!
HE'S CUSTOMIZED YOU LOOK YOU STARE!!

A Slant To Eyes A Beauty Rare!!!
So Don't You Think Know Don't You Know!!
I've Hid In Him A Buddhist Glow!!
Yes Other Faiths I Know He Be!!
But Buddha's Large In Family Tree!!
So Keep Your Eyes Yes Open Wide!!
Cause Asian Wealth Is Gift To Fly!!!
The Dragon's Real Inside His Heart
A Destiny In God Is ART!!!

Jesus

Rosa Parks

Note: Woke Up 4:38am
Rosa Parks was in my bedroom standing on the right side of my headboard. She softly was waking me up to give me a writing. So sweet to me, told me she loved me and was sorry to wake me up.

Said, "The Social Reformers Are Here Julie Please Write For Us."

Rosa Had On Glasses, Coat, and Hat that she was Famous For Wearing. She Looked about 30 years old.

On Back Of Bus You Know I Sat
Enslaved I Be Know Can't Have That!!!
I Had A Heart In Time Was Tuned
"The Water Fountain"!! "No Bathroom"!!!
Cause Black Our Skin And Black Our Hair!!
The Penalty, "No Bed!!! Not Here!!"
Some Doors Were Locked You Know To Us!!
I Thought Of This, "On Back Of Bus"!!!!
So Move I Did!!!! Yes Move Ahead!!
And Lifted High A "Woman's!!! Head!!!"
A Martyr Was You Know That Day
But Life Of Shame We Lived In Grey!!
So Brought I Did A Brighter Light

To See Us Clear!!! The Black!!! The White!!!
In Heaven Now I Have A View!!!
I Love You All Respect I Do!!!
So Say My Name!!!! You Know I'm There
To Answer Call To Answer Prayer!!!

Love, Rosa

Love To You All Forever!!!

I Live For Love!!!!!

Mother Teresa

Note: Woke up 5:35am
Mother Teresa was standing at left of my bed with John Lennon, Abraham Lincoln, Gandhi, Michael Jackson and others, couldn't see clearly.

Kept seeing flashes of them. Hearing spiritual sound bites like so many writings were coming in at once. So I just laid in my bed till I heard someone speak a little clearer, louder than the rest.

Mother Teresa was the strongest voice!!!

Sounds corny but they were all singing, "We Are The World."

Possibly You Know I'm Rare!!
An Angel Here An Angel There!!
I Heal The Sick I Heal The Poor!!
I Open Eyes In God Adore!!
The Penalty I Had On Earth Was Destitute
They Had No Worth!!
The Pain They Lived It Filled Me Large!!!
I Must Set Free Know Free Of Charge!!!
So Roamed The Earth I Begged I Did!!!
So Rich Would Open Eyes And Give!!!
Cause Bottle Wine He Drinks It Rare!!
Could Feed The Poor A Month With Care!!!

Mother Teresa

WILLIAM JEFFERSON CLINTON

NOTE: 8:43AM
BILL CLINTON WAS IN MY BEDROOM LAST NIGHT MAYBE
3AM OR SO, WAS SO TIRED JUST COULD NOT PHYSICALLY GET
OUT OF BED TO TAKE A WRITING. JUST HOPED HE WOULD
COME LATER WHEN I WAS AWAKE.

WELL, THIS MORNING AS I WAS MAKING MY BED I SAW
HIS SOUL AGAIN, HOLDING A NOTE PAD AND A PEN AND
SAID, "WRITE FOR ME NOW, PLEASE DARLIN'."

THIS IS WHAT HE SAID.

I AM A MAN WITH TAINTED PAST
UNFAITHFUL MAN WITH WIFE LOW CLASS!!
BUT WANT YOU SEE AND WANT YOU KNOW
I LIVED ON "CREDIT CARD" OF "SHOW"!!
I SHOWED THE WORLD I SHOWED THEM HIGH
THE HURT THE PAIN REJECTION WIFE!!
I HAD AN ANGEL KNOW I DID
BUT SNUCK AROUND WITH WOMAN "HID"!!
THE GAME GAVE PLEASURE MINUTE, MORE
THEN PUT ON CLOTHES WALKED OUT THE DOOR!!
BUT DIRTY WAS MY LIFE MY HEAD
JUST FILLED WITH LIES AND "SHAME" AND DREAD!!!
SEE LAWS YOU BREAK YOU PAY A PRICE
THE PENALTY OF SELFISH VICE!!
SO CLEAN IT UP YOU HAVE TO MUST!!
SO LOVE CAN HEAL AND FILL WITH TRUST!!!
CAUSE ROTTEN FLOOR YOU'LL WALK ON HOUSE
IF FILLED WITH "ILLS" MUST THROW THEM OUT!!!

BILL

Anne Frank

NOTE: 4:03AM
WOKE UP, ANNE FRANK WAS STANDING AT THE END OF MY
BED HOLDING A LIGHT PURPLE FLOWER.

ASKED ME SWEETLY TO WRITE FOR HER, SO I WENT IN
THE LIVING ROOM AND SAT IN MY "PRAYER CHAIR" AND
WAITED FOR HER TO SPEAK (KEPT SEEING FLASHES OF HER
IN MY LIVING ROOM STANDING IN FRONT OF ME).

THIS IS WHAT SHE SAID.

P.S. FEEL SO HONOURED THAT SHE IS IN MY HOUSE RIGHT
NOW.

MY NAME WAS ANNE!! THE LIFE I LIVED
WAS FILLED WITH WONDER AS A KID!!
I PLAYED WITH DOLLS I RAN OUTSIDE
I ATE GOOD FOOD WAS FULL INSIDE!!
BUT WAR IT CAME IT BLASTED THROUGH!!!
AND TORE UP LOVELY LIFE MY VIEW!!
THE HATE TOWARD ME A JEWISH GIRL!!!
WAS AGONY I LOST MY TWIRL!!!
CAUSE DANCE YOU SEE WAS IN MY HEART
A SONG INSIDE MY HOUSE AND ART!!
BUT WAR OF RACE THE EVIL FELT!!!
THEY LOCKED US UP IN TORTURE CELLS!!!
MY THOUGHTS YOU KNOW BEFORE I DIED
WERE FILLED WITH PRAYER TO GOD I CRIED!!!
"PLEASE MAKE THE EARTH TO UNDERSTAND

THE WEALTH INSIDE EACH LOVELY MAN!!
AWAKEN HEART TO TRULY SEE
THE BEAUTY LOVE IN GIRL LIKE ME!!!
CAUSE WONDERED MUCH SO COLD AND SCARED
HOW PLAGUE INFECTED MINDS "AWARE"!!!
SO FILLED WITH HATE YOU KNOW THEY WERE!!
THE LOWEST RUNG OUR CELLS OUR FLOOR!!!
WE SAT AROUND IN MISERY
AND TALKED OF LIFE THAT USED TO BE!!!
OUR HOPES THEY LEFT OUR HOPES THEY DIED
AS GASSED US EACH OUR WILL SURVIVE!!!
WE WANTED MUCH THE WAR TO END
BUT HELL ETERNAL WAS OUR FRIEND!!!
WE CRIED TO GOD WITH ALL OUR MIGHT!!!
HE HEARD US NOT SO FAITH IT DIED!!
BUT NOW IN HEAVEN HIGH YOU SEE!!!
AM FILLED WITH LOVE AND LIGHT AM FREE!!!!
SO LESSON GIVE YES LESSON LEARNED
MUST LOVE EACH OTHER FULL AND BURN!!!
WITH BEAUTY DIFFERENT EVERY FLOWER
A MEDICINE IN RACES POWER!!!
SEE ANTIDOTE TO HEAL THE WORLD
IS GOLD INSIDE THE DIFFERENT PEARLS!!!

LOVE ANNE

LOVE ONE ANOTHER PLEASE!!!

ALL YOU NEED IS LOVE!!!

John And Jackie

Note: 9:39am
After writing from Bill Clinton, kept seeing flashes of Jackie Kennedy and John F. Kennedy in my living room. The President is wearing a White Tux and Tails, The First Lady Is Wearing Her Hair Gracefully in a "Chignon", White Gloves past her elbow and beautiful gown with little diamonds on it. Tiny delicate Tiara in hair.

Looks like they were at some Royal Party in Heaven and stepped out for a minute to give me this "Writing".

(Feel a little underdressed sitting here with messy hair and pyjamas on.)

A Famous Man You Know I Was
I Had A Name With Fame A "Cause"!!
I Opened Eyes To Racial Pleas!!
I Helped The Poor I Wanted Free!!
Cause Poverty It Has "No Place!!!"
In Country Called "United States!!!!"
My Wife She Came With Me A "Pair"
You liked The Way We Looked You "Stared!!"
Cause "Perfect Match" We Seemed To Be
But I Was "Ill" Fidelity!!
I Played The Field I Played It Hard
The "Conquests" Filled My Dance My Card!!
How Wrong I Was I See It Now
The Nights She'd "Weep To Sleep!!!", "My Foul"!!!

158

I Broke The Laws Of Marriage See
So Selfish Ego Man Was Me!!

Love, Jack

Helen Keller

Note: 10:38am
Thought I was going to "Church" this morning but
keep seeing "People from Heaven" in my house!! Was
washing my dishes when saw Helen Keller in front
of me, then she started speaking this writing to me.
Here it is.

The Blindness In My Eyes You See!!!
Is Special Sight!!! "The Poor" Set Free!!!
I Saw Unfairness Everywhere The "Handicapped"
The "Shame" They Bear!!!
See Special Mission Was My Life!!!
I Showed The Strength In Woman "High!!!"
Cause Pain Was Heavy "Carried Cross"
Of Blindness!!! Deafness!! Muteness!!! Talk!!!
But Learn I Did To Read And Write
And Speak Of Freedom Souls Bring Light!!!
Cause Angel Am In Heaven High!!!
I Came To Earth To Teach You Fly!!!!

Love, Helen

Open The Eyes Of Your Heart!!!

Eleanor Roosevelt

NOTE: 3:53AM

Woke up seeing flashes of Eleanor Roosevelt at the foot of my bed. Kept trying to go back to sleep, but Eleanor was so persistent that I wake up to take a writing. I thought she was going to give me the writing but I was wrong. As I walked into the living room to receive from "Eleanor" I saw flashes of The First Lady Rosalynn Carter, it was her soul that wanted to speak to me.

P.S. Knew that Rosalynn had been, and is, an Advocate for the "Mentally Ill" but didn't know that she was the Second First Lady To Speak to Congress on behalf of her "Cause". Eleanor Roosevelt was the "First"!!! She had been an Advocate for Human Rights of All sorts!!

(Two Powerful Women in my house at once!! Feel part of History right now somehow.)

A Mental Illness Lady Am!!!
I've Opened Eyes To "Pain Within"!!!!
A Martyr's Life You Have To Know!!!
A Blackened Spot On Family Glow!!!
As Younger Woman Yes I Cared
For "Throwaways" The "Thought Impaired"!!!!
So Listen To Me Listen Now!!!
They're Saints On High Must Take A Bow!!!!!
Cause Take The "Family Pain" They do!!!!
Misunderstood God's Special Crew!!!!

Love, Rosalynn

THOMAS EDISON

NOTE: 3:16AM
WOKE UP, WAS READING BIBLE ON MY IPHONE WHEN BATTERY DIED. WAS KIND OF IN A PANIC BECAUSE I LEFT MY CHARGER AT WORK (BIBLE HELPS ME SLEEP). THEN REMEMBERED THAT MY STEREO CAN CHARGE MY PHONE. AS I KNELT DOWN TO CLICK PHONE INTO THE STEREO, LOOKED UP AND SAW THOMAS EDISON STANDING ABOVE ME. HIS LEFT HAND WAS A HUGE LIGHT BULB. WAS WEARING SUIT FROM TURN OF THE CENTURY.
STARTED SPEAKING THIS WRITING TO ME.

YOU HAVE TO KNOW I PAID THE PRICE
TO BRING THE WORLD TO GIVE IT LIGHT!!
A CHOSEN MAN I WAS BECAUSE
I WORKED ALL DAY AND NIGHT NO LAWS!!!
CAUSE COULD NOT SLEEP HAD SPINNING WHEELS
INVENTION THOUGHTS WERE GIVEN THRILLS!!!
SO IMPLEMENT I TRIED I DID
TENACIOUS MAN WAS HOW I LIVED!!!
SO DON'T GIVE UP KNOW HAVE TO FIGHT!!!
TO LIVE YOUR DREAM YES LIVE IN LIGHT!!!

LOVE, THOMAS EDISON

KEEP THE FAITH!!

NEVER GIVE UP!!!

HOPE!!!

DREAM!!!

ACHIEVE!!!

Abraham Lincoln

Had been asleep for about an hour then woke up starving!!

As I was making myself a little snack I saw a flash of Abe Lincoln standing in the kitchen area.

Started hearing him speak this writing to me. Ran to get a book and pen. Here it is.

Apparently You Know I'm Rare
A Noble Man The Pain I Bare!!
The Civil War It Came A Time!!
The Women Screamed, "Give Us Our Dime!!"!!
Cause Voice They Shared It Grew You See!!
Just Want The Vote The Rights Of "She!!"!!
But Had A Choice I Did I Do
To Focus Light On Racial View!!!
Cause Slaves We Had The Sin A Crime!!!!!
We Hung Them Dead On Trees On Vines!!!
So Heaviness In Heart We Felt
When Nation Lived With Whips And Welts!!!
So Freedom Came It Had To Know!!!
To Break The Curse!!! The Slaves Let Go!!!!

Love, Abe

Had To Set Our Country Free!!!!

Break The Curse!!!!

Bring In The Light!!!!

Jackie Chan

NOTE: 9:06AM
SAW KARATE KID MOVIE LAST NIGHT. JACKIE CHAN HAS BEEN IN MY HOUSE ALL NIGHT AND MORNING (SPEAKING WISDOMS TO ME).

WAS BRUSHING MY TEETH WHEN THIS WRITING STARTED COMING IN.

I SENT HIM THERE YOU KNOW I DID
TO OPEN EYES TO ANCIENT GRID!!
THE PATHWAYS TRUE YOU UNDERSTAND
A SPECIAL GUIDE TO HEAVEN'S LAND!!
HE PLAYS A FOOL SO MUCH YOU SEE
A TYPE OF BAIT SO EGO FREE!!
CAUSE MASTER PLAN I HAVE INSIDE
THIS "CHINA MAN" A "SPIRIT GUIDE"!!
HE'LL TAKE YOU HIGH HE'LL TAKE YOU LOW
TO SHOW YOU WEAKNESS TEACH TO GROW!!
MUST OPEN EYES OF LOVE BEWARE
A FLOOD OF ANCIENT BLESSINGS THERE!!!!!

LOVE, JESUS

ANCIENT WISDOMS!!!!!

CHINA!!!!

William Shakespeare

NOTE: 11:12PM
WAS DRIVING HOME FROM WORK KEPT SEEING FLASHES OF "SHAKESPEARE" SITTING IN THE PASSENGER SEAT OF MY CAR. HE KEPT SPEAKING WRITINGS TO ME. I THOUGHT IT WAS ODD BEING THAT I WAS DRIVING ON THE FREEWAY WITHOUT A PEN OR A BOOK TO WRITE DOWN WHAT HE WAS SAYING. I KEPT SEEING FLASHES OF HIM AS I WAS GETTING READY FOR BED. NOT SURE IF I WAS SUPPOSED TO WRITE HIS MESSAGE OR NOT.

WAS SITTING DOWN CHECKING MY E-MAILS WHEN BAM!! I SAW HIM SO STRONG STANDING IN FRONT OF ME AND HEARD THIS WRITING LOUD!! HERE IS WHAT "MASTER" WILLIAM SHAKESPEARE SAID.

A FAMOUS MAN I WAS BACK WHEN
I INKED MY BOOKS WITH FEATHER PENS!!
I WROTE OF LOVE I WROTE OF FIGHTS
I WROTE OF DYNASTIES AND KNIGHTS!!
MY PEN WAS SHARP I HAD A WIT
IT SPOKE TO AUDIENCE A BIT!!
SO I WILL TELL YOU THIS I WILL
THE LANGUAGE ENGLISH GAVE ME THRILLS!!!
CAUSE PLAY WITH WORDS MY GAME WAS FINE!!
I'D HIDE MY SECRETS BETWEEN THE LINES!!!
SO CLEVER WOVEN HISTORY TALES
WOULD TALK TO ROME AND SHAKE HER BELLS!!
CAUSE CHURCH IT HAD A HOLD SO TIGHT

TO CHOKE THE WORLD AND TAKE HER RIGHTS!!!

LOVE, WILLIAM

FREEDOM THROUGH THE PEN!!!

OPEN THE EYES OF THE "MASSES"!!

William Shakespeare "Knight"

NOTE: 1:26AM
WOKE UP FROM A DEEP SLEEP, FELT A POWER SURGING ALL OVER MY BODY, ESPECIALLY IN MY ARMS AND HANDS. FELT SO STRONG TO GET OUT OF BED, GET ON KNEES TO PRAY.

AS I WAS PRAYING I SAW SHOES BY MY FACE ON THE FLOOR. IT WAS WILLIAM SHAKESPEARE AGAIN.

STARTED HEARING THIS WRITING, GRABBED A BOOK TO WRITE IN. HERE IT IS.

I'M GOOD, I'M BAD, I'M IN BETWEEN
YOU WONDER WHY MY STORIES BEAM??!!
I HAVE TO TELL YOU HERE TONIGHT
THE MESSAGE CLEAR I AM A KNIGHT!!!!
I FIGHT FOR LOVE FOR FAIRNESS LAND
FOR EQUAL RIGHTS YOU UNDERSTAND!!!
THE TAMING OF THE SHREW YOU KNOW
WAS IMAGE OF A FIGHTER SHOW!!!!
I LIVED IN TIME OH CAN'T YOU SEE
YOU TAMED A HORSE AND WOMAN THEE!!!!
CAUSE REBEL NOT OH CAN'T YOU SEE
MUST TAKE HER THOUGHTS MOLEST HER "FREE"!!!
FOR PRISONER A WOMAN WAS
SHE HAD NO RIGHTS NO VOICE BECAUSE
A MAN WAS STRONG YOU UNDERSTAND

He Owned The Title To The Land!!!
So Work For Him She Will She Must
Or Discard Find Another "Bust"!!!

Love William

Human Rights Advocate!!!

Believe It!!!!

General William Sherman

NOTE: 2:37AM
WAS TRYING REAL HARD TO GO BACK TO SLEEP BUT KEPT SEEING FLASHES OF GENERAL SHERMAN WALKING THROUGH MY BED AND PACING AROUND MY BEDROOM. HE SEEMED READY TO GIVE ME A WRITING. HERE IT IS.

I AM A MAN YOU UNDERSTAND
I FOUGHT FOR GOD TO FREE THE LAND!!
THE STAKES WERE HIGH THE STAKES WERE LOW
WE HAD TO FREE THE SLAVES YOU KNOW!!
OUR LAND WAS FREE OR SO THEY SAY
BUT RAPED AND BEAT THE "BLUES" AND "GREY"!!
SEE LINES WERE DRAWN IN LAND OF FREE!!
BUT FAIRNESS LITTLE "BLACK" OR "SHE"!!!!
KNOW WOMEN'S MOVEMENT WAS AT HAND
THE "SUFFRAGETTE" SHE "STORMED" THE LAND!!
CAUSE SLAVES THEY CAME IN DIFFERENT FORMS
OUR NATION SICK SO FILLED WITH HARM!!!!
SO FOUGHT WE DID TO BRING IN LIGHT!!
TO FREE THE SHACKLED TREAT THEM RIGHT!!!

SERVANT OF GOD!!!

WILLIAM SHERMAN

Sir Edmund Hillary

Note: 4:22am
Sir Edmund Hillary has been in my house for the past few days. Finally gave me a writing this morning!!! Edmund is the first to reach the summit of Mount Everest along with his Legendary Sherpa Guide Tenzing Norgay!!! Following his Ascent of Everest He Devoted much of His Life to Helping The Sherpa People.

I Need To Tell You This I Will!!!
I've Climbed Up Mountains "Big"!!!! My Thrill!!!!
Was Sent To Earth To Soar To Fly!!!
To Teach The Soul Don't Give Up Try!!!
Tenacious Man I Was You Know!!!
Explorer Plan Was How I'd Go!!!!
I Reached The Poles!!! The Heights On Earth!!!!
Then Teach The "Man" To Give His Worth!!!
Cause Way To Make The Low Place Gone!!!
To Bring Your Soul To Joy And Song!!!
Is Climb Through Life In Charity!!!!
Open Heart To Giving Thee!!!

Love, Edmund Hillary

Give Much!!!

Reward Much!!!

Joy!!! Peace!!! Happiness!!!

KATHARINE HEPBURN

NOTE: 9:53AM
LAST NIGHT ABOUT 3:52AM, I WAS TRYING TO GO BACK TO
SLEEP AFTER TAKING WRITINGS FROM SHAKESPEARE AND
SHERMAN. I WAS SO TIRED I FELT LIKE I WAS GOING TO
COLLAPSE, JUST FALL APART!!

THESE WRITINGS DRAIN MY BODY AND MY SOUL
SOMEHOW. IT'S LIKE SURGES OF ENERGY BLASTING IN
AND OUT OF MY BODY. I WAS JUST DOZING OFF WHEN
"THE GREATEST AMERICAN ACTRESS OF THE CENTURY"!!!
"KATHARINE HEPBURN" REVEALED HERSELF NEXT TO MY
BED. SHE WAS SPEAKING TO ME WITH HER BEAUTIFUL
VOICE!! COULD SEE AND HEAR HER SO CLEAR!!! KNEW
SHE WANTED ME TO TAKE A WRITING FOR HER BUT I JUST
COULDN'T TAKE IT. WOKE UP THIS MORNING AND SAW A
FLASH OF HER IN THE KITCHEN. SHE STARTED SPEAKING
THIS WRITING TO ME.

THIS IS WHAT SHE SAID.

MY NAME IS GREAT OH CAN'T YOU SEE??!!
A FAMOUS ACTRESS YES I BE!!!!
THE STRENGTH INSIDE MY SOUL WAS RIGHT!!!!
TO TELL THE STORIES "WOMAN'S PLIGHT"!!!
I WALKED ON EARTH I WALKED REAL "TALL"
AND OPENED DOORS "RESPECT" AND "AWE"!!!!!
CAUSE ELEGANCE I CARRIED PROUD!!!!
WITH DIGNITY MY "TALK" WAS LOUD!!!!
I SPOKE OF LOVE I SPOKE OF PAIN!!!!
I SPOKE TO "MEN", "RESPECT"!!! MY "NAME"!!!!!

Cause "Women's Advocate" I Was
Just Open "Eyes" See "Stars" Above!!!!

Love, Katharine

Movie Stars!!!!

Messengers!!! Heal The World!!!!!

John Wayne

NOTE: 4:27AM

WAS FALLING ASLEEP LAST NIGHT AND SAW JOHN WAYNE. HE WALKED THROUGH MY BALCONY DOOR AND WALKED STRAIGHT THROUGH MY WALL INTO MY BEDROOM. HAD HIS FACE TO MY FACE. HE TOLD ME HE LOVED ME AND WOULD WAKE ME UP LATER TO GIVE ME A WRITING. HE DID AND HERE IT IS.

P.S. JOHN WAYNE DIED OF LUNG CANCER AND STOMACH CANCER AT 75 YEARS OLD. SMOKED SIX PACKS OF CIGARETTES A DAY.

A MARLBORO MAN I SEEMED TO BE!!
I SMOKED AND DRANK, "PHILOSOPHY"!!
BUT DON'T YOU SEE I PAID THE PRICE
OF LIVING LIFE YES FILLED WITH VICE!!
THE "BIG STRONG MAN", I WALKED REAL "TALL"
BUT CIGARETTE IT MADE ME FALL!!
I AGED REAL FAST!!!! IN POISON BED
I FELL ASLEEP WITH DRUNKEN HEAD!!
AN ADDICT WAS MOST OF MY LIFE!!!
UNHEALTHY SICK I'D CHANGE IT "NICE"!!!
I'D RUN TO STORE GET HELP YOU SEE
I'D WEAR THE PATCH TO SET ME FREE!!!!
CAUSE CIGARETTE IT TASTED "GOOD"!!!
BUT PRISON WARDEN!! PRISON FOOD!!!
SO LISTEN TO ME, LISTEN NOW!!!
GIVE UP UNHEALTHY WEDDING VOW!!

Cause Marriage To UnHealthy Life
Is Misery A Life Of Strife!!!!

Love, John Wayne

Be Healthy!!!

Be Strong!!!!

Be Happy!!!!!

RUSSELL CROWE

NOTE: 11:30AM
WOKE UP. STARTED WALKING INTO THE KITCHEN AND HAD
RUSSELL CROWE WALKING AROUND MY HOUSE. FELT HIM
WALK THROUGH ME A COUPLE OF TIMES (ENERGY SURGES)!!
HIS SOUL STARTED SPEAKING TO ME RIGHT AWAY. FELT LIKE
HE HAD TO RUSH AND GIVE ME A WRITING. VERY!! VERY!!
STRONG!!! PRESENCE!!! GIANT!!!!!
   (I SAW ROBIN HOOD LAST NIGHT, AT THEATRE.)

AMAZING MAN I SEEM TO BE!!!
I PLAY THE "FIGHTER" WITHIN "THEE"!!!!!
BUT "WEAK" INSIDE I HAVE THAT TOO!!!
AS HUMAN MAN I STRUGGLE THROUGH!!!
BUT HAVE A HEART SO BIG SO LARGE!!!
IT MATCHES UP MY FIGHT MY CAUSE!!!
I'LL BRING THE EARTH AN INSIGHT FREE!!!
TO FIGHT YOUR "DEMONS!!!", "MERRY BE!!!"
CAUSE RIGHTEOUS "MAN" I PLAY I "AM"!!!!!
I FIGHT FOR TRUTH AND FAIRNESS LAND!!!!
SO LOVE ME PLEASE YOU CAN YOU WILL!!!
I'M "FRIEND OF THEE AN "AUSSIE!!!", "THRILL!!!"

LOVE, RUSSELL

DON'T GIVE UP!!!

FIGHT!!!!

WIN!!!!!

PROSPER!!!!

LIVE BIG!!!!!

LOVE LARGE!!!!!!

PERSIAN WOMEN!!

NOTE: 8:56AM
HAD DREAM LAST NIGHT THAT I WAS BACK IN IRAN.
WALKING WITH HUNDREDS OF PERSIAN WOMEN. WE
WERE CLIMBING A MOUNTAIN!! MANY CHILDREN WERE
CLIMBING WITH US!! DIDN'T SEE ANY MEN.

FELT SO JOYOUS!! ALL THE WOMEN WERE SINGING AND
LAUGHING!! SO HAPPY!! SOMEHOW, I KNEW THAT WE
WERE CLIMBING OUT OF "DARKNESS", "OPPRESSION", INTO
"FREEDOM", "HUMAN RIGHTS"!!

FELT A LOVE FOR THESE WOMEN SO STRONG!! WAS
CRYING IN MY "DREAM" HAD TEARS ON MY FACE WHEN
I WOKE UP!! MY BEDROOM WAS FILLED WITH IRANIAN
WOMEN CLAPPING AROUND MY BED!!!

THIS IS THE WRITING THEY GAVE ME.

I NEED TO SHOUT AND MAKE IT CLEAR!!!
THE TIME FOR PERSIAN POWER HERE!!!!
MY COUNTRY'S FILLED WITH LIES DECEIT!!!
OPPRESS THE PEOPLE MOSTLY "SHE'S"!!!!
WE WEAR OUR VEILS WE WEAR THEM RIGHT!!!
JUST SHOW A BIT OF HAIR!!! DON'T SLIDE!!!!
CAUSE IF YOU SEE OUR "HAIR!!! ADORNED!!!"
A PENALTY FOR US OF "SCORN!!!"
SO LOOK AT ME I WANT YOU TO!!!!
I'M "EDUCATED!!!","LANGUAGE TOO!!!!"
A FLUENT TONGUE I HAVE YOU SEE!!!
IT'S FILLED WITH "FAITH" IN "WOMAN"!!!"ME!!!"

So Watch Us Close!! I Know You Will
As Overthrow!!!! The "Prison!!!!!","Veil!!!"

Love, Women Of Iran

Freedom!!!!

Rights!!!! Choice!!!!

WOMEN OF THE HOLOCAUST

NOTE: 2:34AM
A FEW DAYS AGO WOMEN OF THE HOLOCAUST STARTED
SHOWING THEMSELVES TO ME. THEN ONE NIGHT IT WAS
CHILDREN OF THE HOLOCAUST!! TONIGHT IT IS BOTH.
HERE IS THE WRITING FROM THE WOMEN. (MY HOUSE IS
FILLED WITH THEM RIGHT NOW!!)

THEY SHAVED OUR HEADS OH CAN'T YOU SEE??
THE "WOMAN CONCENTRATION CAMP" WAS "ME"!!!
WE SUFFERED MUCH YOU KNOW WE DID!!!
IN AGONY WE LOST OUR KIDS!!!
THEY TOOK OUR BABIES FROM OUR "ARMS"
DECAPITATED FILLED WITH HARMS!!!
OUR HUSBANDS YES, THEY TOOK THEM TOO!!!
OUR DIGNITY OUR HOPEFUL VIEW!!!
WE LOST IT ALL WERE STRIPPED SO BARE!!!
WE PRAYED TO GOD HE SHOWED NO CARE!!!
THE JEWISH MARTYR THAT WAS "ME"!!!
A MOTHER'S HEART TO WEEP AND BLEED!!!
REPAIR FOR US A WORLD WIDE VIEW!!!
AS DICTATE TO YOU WORD OR TWO!!!!
OUR MESSAGE CLEAR!!! OUR MESSAGE LIGHT!!!
MUST FREE "THE WOMAN" SUFFER, "RIGHTS"!!!
THE HIGHEST VOICE WE HAVE YOU SEE!!!!
A SPIRIT POWER WOMAN THEE!!!

WE TOOK THE PAIN IN PAST WE DID!!!!
TO OPEN GATES OF LOVE TO LIVE!!!

LOVE, HOLOCAUST ANGELS

HELP THE POOR!!!!

HEAL THE WORLD!!!

Albert Einstein

NOTE: 8:31AM
LAST NIGHT SAW FLASHES OF "EINSTEIN" BEFORE GOING
TO SLEEP. WOKE UP THIS MORNING AND WAS CLEANING
THE HOUSE WHEN I SAW HIM IN MY BEDROOM DOORWAY,
STARTED SPEAKING THIS "WRITING" TO ME.

A MIRACLE I GAVE TO YOU!!!
A "GENIUS!!!!!", "MAN" MY NAME IS TOO!!!
I WALKED ON EARTH!!!! I WALKED REAL "TALL"!!!!
A "MYSTERY!!!!","MIND!!!!" I HAD IT ALL!!!!
JUST TOUCH THE HEM MY ROBE YOU SEE!!!
ILLUMINATION!!! GUST OF "ME!!!"
IMPORTANT "MAN" I WAS IN TIME,
AS JEWISH "MAN" IT WAS A CRIME!!!!!
SO LIFT THE "EYES" YOU KNOW I DID!!!
TO EVERY LITTLE "JEWISH", "KID"!!!!!
PREPARED THE LAND!!! PREPARED THEM RIGHT!!!
SEE "JEWISH", "STAR!!!" I BROUGHT "DELIGHT"!!!!

LOVE, ALBERT

JEWISH STARS!!!

JEWS GIFTS FROM HEAVEN!!!!!

SPECIAL GIFTS!!!!

BELIEVE IT!!!!

Vincent van Gogh

NOTE: 8:25AM
WOKE UP THIS MORNING, SAW VINCENT VAN GOGH STANDING BY MY WINDOW HOLDING A BIG BOUQUET OF SUNFLOWERS!!! HE WAS WEARING A HAT TILTED TO THE SIDE, WEARING A GREY SUIT LOOKING VERY HANDSOME, DASHING!!!

THIS IS WHAT HE SAID.

INCREDIBLE I AM YOU KNOW!!!
A VERY SPECIAL ARTIST GLOW!!!
I PAINTED FAST I PAINTED HARD!!!
IT HELPED MY MIND RENEW!!! DISCARD!!!
CAUSE THOUGHTS WERE HEAVY!!!
THOUGHTS WERE RARE!!!
IN DARKEST PLACES PAIN WAS THERE!!!!
I SUNK DOWN DEEP I TRIED TO SWIM!!!
THE PAINTBRUSH!!! PALLET!!! WERE MY FINS!!!!
SO STROKE I DID EXPLOSIVE MAN!!!
THE SWIRLS OF LIGHT DELIGHTED AM!!!
BUT AGONY I LIVED IN MUCH!!!
A HEIGHTENED MAN REFINED MY TOUCH!!!
I HAD TO OPEN DOORS YOU SEE!!!!
THE "ARTIST", "PAINT" ARE SPIRIT KEYS!!!!

FREEDOM THROUGH ART!!!
LIVE OUTSIDE THE LINES!!!!
DRAW YOUR OWN LINES!!!!
CHOICES!!!!
FREEDOM!!!!
POWER!!!!

Sephardic Angel

NOTE: 8:42AM
LAST NIGHT I KEPT SEEING FLASHES OF AN ANCIENT LOOKING JEWISH MAN STANDING IN FRONT OF ME.

I WAS READING A BOOK IN MY LIVING ROOM AND KEPT DOZING OFF, SAW HIM STANDING IN FRONT OF ME SEVERAL TIMES. KEPT HEARING THE WORD "SEPHARDIC" OVER AND OVER.

I HAD MET WITH A FRIEND EARLIER IN THE DAY AND SHE IS FROM A "SEPHARDIC" BACKGROUND.

I ASSUME THIS SEPHARDIC ANGEL IS CONNECTED TO HER!!

I HAD THE BEST NIGHT SLEEP LAST NIGHT!!! NORMALLY I HAVE TO WAKE UP AND PRAY SEVERAL TIMES THROUGH THE NIGHT, BUT WHEN "ELI" REVEALED HIMSELF AGAIN TO ME THIS MORNING I REALIZED THAT HE BLESSED MY HOME LAST NIGHT!!!! (REALLY INTERESTED IN SEPHARDIC JEWS RIGHT NOW!!)

THIS IS THE WRITING HE GAVE ME.

A MAN SEPHARDIC THAT IS ME!!!
I PRAY FOR PEOPLE SAD THEY BE!!!
I WALK THE STREETS ALL THROUGH THE NIGHTS!!!
I LAY MY HANDS ON HEADS SO RIGHT!!!
CAUSE CARRY BLESSINGS RARE I DO!!!
IF VISITING I GIVE TO YOU!!!
THE PEACE I BRING IS HIGH YOU SEE!!!
CAUSE ANCIENT SOUL OF PRAYER I BE!!!
SO THINK OF ME PLEASE IF YOU CAN!!!
AN ANGEL HIGH AN ANGEL AM!!!

I Visit Realm You Know As Earth!!!
To Lift Up Higher Thoughts And Worth!!!

Thank You, Eli

Jewish Blessings!!!

Jewish Power!!! Peace!!!!

CHRISTOPHER COLUMBUS

NOTE: 4:30AM
WOKE UP A BIT AGO WITH CHRISTOPHER COLUMBUS IN MY BEDROOM. HE WALKED THROUGH THE WALL AND WOKE ME UP TO TAKE A WRITING. HE LOOKS ABOUT 30 YEARS OLD HAS DARK BROWN SHOULDER LENGTH HAIR.

REALLY, REALLY HANDSOME!! WEARING BLACK DOUBLE BREASTED JACKET, BLACK JEANS. SO STYLISH HE LOOKS VERY MODERN, FRENCH/ITALIAN STYLE. HE IS TALL AND SLENDER. JUST BEAUTIFUL!!!

A WORLD YOU SEE YES VERY CLEAR!!!
IS HARD FOR OTHERS BRINGS THEM FEAR!!!!!
AN UNKNOWN LAND YOU GO WHEN "DIE"!!!
IS FULL OF LIFE IN "POWER"!!! "THRIVE"!!!!!
SO SPEAK WITH PEN!!! WE WANT YOU TO!!!
RELEASE THE GEMS OF HIGHER TRUTH!!!!
YOU LIVE ON EARTH IT'S "NICE" WE KNOW!!??
BUT KIND OF "DIRTY" THOUGHTS ARE LOW!!!!
A TIME WILL COME!!!!! IT'S ON ITS WAY!!!
OF HIGHER THOUGHTS!!! A NEW HIGH WAY!!!
YOU'LL LEARN TO PRAY YES REACH THE SKIES!!!
YOU'LL OPEN WINGS!!!! SO YOU CAN FLY!!!!
MUST SEE THE WORLD WITH "BRIGHTER" LIGHT!!!
ERASE THE "DARK"!!! ERASE THE "FRIGHT"!!!
ABOLISH WAR YOU KNOW WE WILL!!!
AND OPEN ARMS WITH LOVE WE'LL FILL!!!!!

LOVE, CHRISTOPHER

THE NEW WORLD!!!!

PEACE!!!!

LOVE!!!!

JOY!!!!!!

CAESAR AUGUSTUS

NOTE: 3:34AM
SO MANY SOULS IN MY HOUSE RIGHT NOW!! STANDING IN FRONT OF ME IS CAESAR AUGUSTUS!!!

He is wearing a long Black Cloak with Gold Trim (embroidery) around the edges.

Underneath is a White Garment so Bright, can't see details only Bright Glare!!

Keep seeing flashes of Him, feel Strong Love Gushing From His Soul!! (Overwhelming)

Apparently I Lived In Time
Dictators Ruled The World "Divine"!!!!
A Man Would Fight A Man Would Live
To Guard His Wife And Guard His Kids!!!!
Cause Never Slept So Still In Bed!!!!
For Thieves Would Come And Steal Our Bread!!!
The Ancient World I Come From Know
Had Poverty A Struggle Low!!!
A Brutal Fight We Breathed In Air!!!!
Not Much Delight Just Hardship There!!!
So Brought The Earth A Balance Fair!!!
"Diplomacy" I Ruled So Rare!!!

Love, Caesar Augustus

CAME TO EARTH TO HELP THE WORLD!!!

VERY HIGH SOUL!!!

KNOW THIS!!!!

MUST KNOW THIS!!!!!

The Holy Prophet Muhammad

NOTE: 5:10AM
WOKE UP HEARING THIS WRITING. MANY, MANY!!! MIDDLE
EASTERN PEOPLE IN MY HOUSE!!!
    OVERWHELMING!!!

I AM A PROPHET DON'T YOU KNOW!!!
HE HOLDS MY KEYS MY GOLDEN GLOW!!!
I CAME TO EARTH YOU KNOW I DID!!!
TO RAISE THE BAR OF HOW WE LIVED!!!
A PAGAN WORLD WAS IN MY TIME!!!
OF SACRIFICE A HUMAN KIND!!!
SO SET IN MOTION SOMETHING NEW!!!
A NEW SENSATION GREW AND GREW!!!!!
THE DOUBT WAS MUCH!!!! A HARD LIFE ME!!!
BUT HAD TO TEACH THE FAITH I SEE!!!!
WAS TORTURED SOUL YOU HAVE TO KNOW!!!!
BUT PURIFIED THE WAY I GO!!!!
MUST UNDERSTAND I KNOW "THE LAMB"
"THE GREATEST GIFT" "THE GREAT I AM"!!!!!
IN HEAVEN NOW WE ALL LIVE FREE!!!!!
RELIGIONS ONE IS ALL WE BE!!!!!

LOVE, MUHAMMAD

ONE PEOPLE!!!!

ONE GOD!!!!

ONE LOVE!!!!!!

Harriet Beecher Stowe

Note: 3:57am
Harriet Beecher Stowe wrote bestselling novel of the 19th century, "Uncle Tom's Cabin".
   Novel influenced the Civil War to begin, The End of Slavery!!!!!
   She is here.

I Wrote A Book You Know I Did!!!
Bout Uncle Tom And How He Lived!!!!
I Lived In Time Was Ripe For Sure!!!
To Freedom Bring!!!! To Slaves A Cure!!!!
So Antidote I Had Through Pen!!!
The Remedy!!! The Page Within!!!
Know Vessel Was I Am For Sure!!!!
To Free The "Black" The "Woman" More!!!
Cause Suffragette I Claim To Be!!!!!
An Advocate From God To Thee!!!
So Say A Prayer Please If You Can!!!!
To Set World Free Of Greedy "Hand"!!!!!
I Have A Sight So Clear I See!!!
With Heaven's Light!!!! The World We'll Feed!!!!!
So Lift Your Eyes Please If You Dare!!!!
Lose Darkness Seed The World Make Fair!!!!!

No More Hunger!!!!

Stop Human Trafficking!!!

Help One Another!!!!!

Please......

Wolfgang Amadeus Mozart

Note: 8:54am
Woke up this morning. Musicians all around my Bed!!! Had seen flashes of souls in Light surrounding my bed the night before but couldn't see them clearly. This morning they showed themselves holding Orchestra Instruments (ALL OF THEM)!!

Mostly seemed to be from the 18th century. Beautiful "Period" clothing. White wigs/hair.

Mozart was sitting at the Piano and started speaking this writing to me.

A Famous Man I Am You See!!
The Ladder Climbed Was High For Me!!!!
A Gift Was Given In My Arms!!
It Flowed Through Fingers "Tickled", "Charmed"!!!
A Royal Man It Seems Am Now!!!
But Struggled Much In Pain Was Thou!!!!
So Lesson Am I'll Give To You!!!
Tenacious Soul Must BULLDOZE Through!!!!
Cause Walls They Come Into Our Life!!!
Must Tear Them Down To Live In Light!!!
Must Love Resistance "Strength" Is There
To Build Us Up To Higher "AIR"!!!!

Love, Wolfgang Amadeus Mozart

NEVER GIVE UP!!!!

OBSTACLES ARE BLESSINGS!!!

CLIMB!!!

LEAP!!!

RUN!!!

FLY!!!!!!

NEVER GIVE UP!!!!

Michael Jackson

NOTE: 5:00AM
WOKE UP STARVING AND MADE A SNACK. THEN FELL TO MY
KNEES IN PRAYER!! POWER SO STRONG SURGING THROUGH
ME!! WALKED INTO THE LIVING ROOM, SAT DOWN AND
STARTED HEARING THIS WRITING COMING IN. GRABBED
A PEN AND BOOK, JUST STARTED WRITING (COULDN'T SEE
WHO IT WAS) AS PEN FLOWED ONTO THE PAPER. HE SHOWED
HIMSELF TO ME, LOOKED ABOUT 30 YEARS OLD WITH LONG
BLACK CURLY HAIR, BLACK LEATHER OUTFIT WITH LOTS
OF ZIPPERS. HIS SKIN WAS CHOCOLATE BROWN, LOOKS SO
HANDSOME!! FELT SO MUCH LOVE IN MY HOUSE!!!

ANOMALY I AM YOU SEE!!!
A PRECIOUS GIFT INSIDE OF THEE!!!
I DANCED YOU KNOW ALL THROUGH THE NIGHT!!!
AS PEOPLE STARED AND WHISPERED HIGH!!!!
CAUSE FAMOUS MAN I WAS YOU KNOW
MY AGE WAS "HID" SO "BRIGHT" MY "GLOW"!!!!!
SO LOVE ME PLEASE!!!! I ASK YOU TO....
FORGIVE "MISTAKE" I HAD A FEW!!!
BUT HUMAN HAND I HAD YOU SEE!!!!
A WEAKER SIDE A VOID IN ME!!!!
CAUSE LOVE WAS THIN AS WAS MY "WORTH"
AS YOUNGER MAN I TRAVELLED EARTH!!!
A SUPER!!!!STAR!!!!! I WAS I AM!!!!
I "ROCKED WITH YOU" AND TAUGHT TO "JAM"!!!!!
SO LISTEN TO ME LISTEN NOW!!!
A SECRET GIVE I WILL IT "THOU"!!!
A JOY IS HIDDEN IN MY WORDS!!

The Notes Of Music "Heal The World"!!!!!
Must Give A Piece Of Rice To Thee!!!!
The "Starving"!!! "Cold"!!!!!! The "Hungry"!!!!"Feed"!!!!
For Then A Joy Will Come To "Land"
A "Freedom"!!!! "Spirit"!!!! "Understand"!!!!
I Love You All!!!! You Know I Do!!!
And Touch You "Will"!!!
Might "DANCE" Through "YOU"!!!!

Love, Michael

Heal The World Make It A Better Place!!!!

GIVE!!!!

HELP!!!!

LOVE..................................

Ludwig van Beethoven

NOTE: 5:42AM
WOKE UP. BEETHOVEN WAS NEXT TO MY BED. WAS SO SLEEPY, VERY HARD TO GET OUT OF BED TO TAKE THIS WRITING!! KEPT FALLING ASLEEP AS I WAS RECEIVING DICTATIONS FROM THE "DEAF" MUSICIAN.
    HERE IS WHAT HE SAID.

MY NAME IS GREAT OH CAN'T YOU SEE??!!
A MUSIC MAN SO HIGH WAS ME!!!
A GIFT WAS GIVEN TO ME LARGE!!!
I TWINKLED KEYS IT GAVE ME CHARGE!!
I LIVED A LIFE IN PAIN YOU SEE!!!!
WHEN LOVE WAS DEEP REJECT WAS ME!!!
THOUGH PAIN WAS GOOD FOR ME MY SOUL!!!
IT BROUGHT ME HIGH RELEASE THE FLOW!!!
CAUSE "CRY" OF SOUL BRINGS ANGELS LARGE!!!!
THEY BROUGHT ME MUSIC SPIRIT "CHARGE"!!!
SO LEGACY YOU SEE IT NOW!!!!
COMPOSED A "GOLDEN" RIVER THOU!!!
CAUSE STREAM OF CONSCIOUSNESS WAS HIGH!!!
SO FILLED WITH WINGS WHERE ANGELS FLY!!!

LOVE, LUDWIG

Listen With Your Heart!!

Music Tunes You Up!!!

Takes Your Soul Higher!!!

Prayer!!!!

Believe It!!!!!!

Pablo Picasso

Note: 4:42am
Just Woke Up!!! Picasso was standing near my bed telling me to wake up!!! Was so tired!!! He said "You Are here to take these writings!!! Born for this!!"

So I got up. This is what he said. (His Presence is so strong in my living room right now!!!!!)

I Came To Earth You Know I Did!!!
To Cause The "Art World" Type of Skid!!!
As Gentle Breeze I Walked Through Halls!!!!
Then Slowly Built Up "Storm"!!! And "Awe"!!!!!
I Twisted "Paintbrush"!!!! Twisted "Pen"!!!!
The "Artist"!!!!"Freed"!!!! From "Cage"!!!!!"Within"!!!!!
I "Speak"!!!!! Yes Volumes With One "Stroke"!!!!!
The Walls Tear Down With Paintbrush "Smote"!!!!!
So Listen Must I Tell You To!!!
A Bit Of "Rush" I Am Get Through!!!!
An "Angel's" Hand I Have You See!!!!!!
My Name's PICASSO That Is ME!!!!!

FOLLOW YOUR HEART!!!

WALK IN TRUTH!!!!

LOVE BIG!!!!

WORK HARD!!!!!

POWER!!!!!

SUCCESS!!!!!!

J.R.R. Tolkien

NOTE: 5:53AM
WOKE UP ABOUT 3:00AM J.R.R. TOLKIEN WAS IN MY
BEDROOM AND WANTED ME TO TAKE A WRITING.
 I WAS SO TIRED I FELL BACK TO SLEEP. THEN WOKE UP
ABOUT 5:45AM, HAD POWERFUL ENERGY ZAPPING THROUGH
MY BODY. GOT UP AND TOOK THIS WRITING. HERE IT IS.

INTELLIGENT I AM YOU KNOW!!!
A SPECIAL MISSION A SPECIAL SHOW!!!
I SPOKE OF LAND CALLED, "MIDDLE EARTH"!!!
THE MESSAGE CLEAR A "SPIRIT WORK"!!!
YOU KNOW A DARK FORCE WAS AT HAND!!!
ALL THROUGH MY LIFE I TOOK A STAND!!!!
CAUSE WANT IT NOW!!!! YOU KNOW I DO!!!!!
THE END OF HATE!!!! RACISM TOO!!!!
CAUSE HEAVEN LIVES AND HEAVEN LOVES!!!!
THE SOLDIERS FIGHT FOR JUSTICE OF.....
THE HUNGRY MAN KNOW MUST HAVE BREAD!!!
THE ORPHAN CHILD A WARM CLEAN BED!!!
SO FOCUS LIFE ON LOVE YOU'LL SEE
A HIGHER EARTH!!!! YOU'LL LIVE THAT'S FREE!!!!

RESPECTFULLY, J.R.R. TOLKIEN

FEED

HELP

LOVE

Judy Garland

Note: 4:04am
Judy Garland woke me up to give me a writing. Here
it is.

A Tragic Life I Lived You See!!!
The "Demon"!!! "Fear"!!!! It Lived In Me!!!!
I Lived A Life Of "Lonely"!!!! "Pain"!!!!!
I'd Seek Applause For Healing "Gain"!!!!
But Needed Healing From Above!!
A Touch From God Of Heaven's Love!!!!
Cause Road I Walked On Filled With "Thorns"!!!!!!
Of Low Esteem So Ripped And Torn!!!!!
So Write My Message Will You Dear!!!
Please Tell The World To "Lose The Fear"!!!!!
Cause Praise And Worship Live Life Right!!!!
Integrity Be Blessed In "Light"!!!!!

Love, Judy

Pray!!!!!

Give!!!!!

Joy!!!!!

Stephen Hawking

NOTE: 3:34AM

JUST WOKE UP A BIT AGO. STEPHEN HAWKING WAS IN A WHEELCHAIR NEXT TO MY BED. KEPT ASKING ME TO PLEASE TAKE A WRITING FOR HIM (I RESISTED, TIRED!!! WENT TO BED LATE). HE STEPPED OUT OF "HIS CHAIR" AND WAS TALL!!! POWERFUL!!! ILLUMINATED!!! WHEN I SAW HIM THAT WAY I THOUGHT "MAYBE I BETTER GET UP AND TAKE THIS WRITING."

MIGHT BE INTERESTING??!! HERE IT IS.

AMAZING MAN YOU KNOW I AM!!!
A "SICKNESS", "BLOW" I DEAL WITH "GLAM"!!!!
INSPIRE MUCH YOU KNOW I DO!!!!
THOUGH "HANDICAPPED" HAVE "HIGHER" VIEW!!!!???
IT SEEMS THAT ALL THE ANSWERS CLEAR!!!!
AN "ATHEIST" A SCHOLAR HERE!!!!
I TELL YOU "DON'T BELIEVE IN GOD"
JUST SCIENCE THOUGHTS!!!!! THE BIG BANG OF!!!!!
RELIGION SEEMS REDUNDANT "THEE"
TO WORSHIP "ONE"!!! OR "TWO"!!! OR "THREE"!!!
BUT HAVE TO KNOW I'LL STIR THE "POT"!!!!
OF SCIENCE "MEN" TO ARGUE!!! TALK!!!
AN INTEREST HIGH FROM WHAT I SAY!!!!
MIGHT POINT TO GOD A "DIFFERENT" WAY!!!!?

LOVE, STEPHEN

GET PEOPLE IRRITATED!!!!

STIMULATED!!!!

POWERFUL!!!!

HEALTHY!!!!

CLEANSING!!!!

Motorcycles

NOTE: 5:10AM
JUST WOKE UP!!! HEARING THIS WRITING SO STRONG!!! HAD ENERGY SURGING THROUGH MY BODY!!! KIND OF JUMPED OUT OF BED TO TAKE THIS WRITING!!! (FROM A DEEP SLEEP)

THERE'S SOMETHING GOT TO MAKE IT CLEAR!!!!
A MOTORCYCLE GOD IS HERE!!!!
I WANT TO SPEAK IT TELL YOU KNOW!!!
YOU FACE YOUR FEARS AND WINGS WILL GROW!!!!
A SPIRIT LIVES INSIDE YOU LARGE
WILL MAGNIFY A SUPER!!!!! CHARGE!!!!!
SO RIDE YOUR BIKE BE SAFE AND SURE!!!!
A SPIRIT "ROCK" WILL BE YOUR "CURE"!!!!

LOVE, JESUS

SUPER!!!! POWER!!!!!

KNOW!!!! THIS!!!!

Children Of The Holocaust

NOTE: 5:17AM
WOKE UP CHILDREN OF THE HOLOCAUST WERE AROUND MY BED!!! ILLUMINATED!!!!!

THE HOLOCAUST WAS PLAIN TO SEE!!!!
THE MURDER OF THE WEAK IN NEED!!!
THE HANDICAPPED KNOW DIDN'T CARE!!!
JUST "THROW"!!!! "DISCARD"!!!! NO GUILT TO "SPARE"!!!!
CAUSE RADICAL THE TIME WAS THEN!!!!
EXTERMINATE IN CAGES!!!! PENNED!!!!
CRY IN THE NIGHT THE CHILDREN PRAYED!!!!
RELEASE FROM FOG THE HATE IN PLAY!!!!
CAUSE FEAR THE DARK YOU KNOW IT WAS!!!!
A GODLESS PLACE "PURE" LACK OF LOVE!!!!
SO WRITE THIS DOWN WE ASK YOU PLEASE!!!
THE "CHILDREN HOLOCAUST" IN HEAVEN PLEAD!!!!
KNOW HEAVEN HIGH WE LIVE THERE NOW!!!!
IN JOY WE LIVE FORGIVEN THOU!!!!!
CAUSE SEE THROUGH "DARKNESS" TIME WE LIVED!!!!
SO HIGH OUR "CROWNS" WHEN WE FORGIVE!!!!

CHILDREN OF THE HOLOCAUST

MUST FORGIVE TO BE FREE!!!!!
FORGIVE ALL!!!!!
LOVE ALL!!!!!!!
NO MATTER WHAT!!!!!!
FREEDOM!!!!!!!!!!!!!!!!!!!

John Fitzgerald Kennedy

NOTE: 8:19AM
WOKE UP ABOUT 3:00AM, HAD JUST HAD "HEAVEN" EXPERIENCE WITH J.F.K. HE WAS SPEAKING TO WHAT SEEMED TO BE THOUSANDS OF "KENNEDY'S". HE WAS GIVING A POWERFUL SPEECH ON "FREEDOM"!!!!

JOLTED AWAKE AND SAW J.F.K. STANDING NEXT TO MY BED. HE SAID HE WOULD GIVE ME THE "WRITING" IN THE MORNING, TOLD ME TO "GO BACK TO SLEEP". HE IS HERE NOW. THIS IS THE WRITING.

WE'RE KENNEDY'S WE TRAVEL FAR!!!!
WE LIFT UP HOW YOU SEE "THE BAR"!!!!!
CAUSE THOUGHTS WERE LOW YOU KNOW BACK WHEN!!!!!!
ON "BACK OF BUS" THE PEOPLE "PENNED"!!!!
WE SAW A MIGHTY SUPER STAR!!!!!
HIS NAME WAS "KING" HE SPOKE WE "AWED"!!!!!
FOR CHOSEN "MAN" HE WAS YOU SEE!!!!
JUST LIKE MY BROTHER "BOBBY"!!!!! "ME"!!!!!!
KNOW ADVOCATES WE SPOKE REAL "HIGH"!!!!
LET'S STOP THE "HATE"!!!! THE PAINFUL CRIES!!!!
CAUSE JUSTICE COMES FROM "HEAVEN" SEE
IN PACKAGES LIKE "MARTIN"!!!! "ME"!!!!!!

LOVE, JACK

CHOSEN SOULS

ILLUMINATED LIFE

ILLUMINATED VOICE

King Joseph Stalin

NOTE: 8:31AM
JOSEPH STALIN HAS BEEN IN MY HOUSE THE PAST TWO DAYS.
SHOWED HIMSELF TO ME THIS MORNING AND SPOKE
THIS WRITING TO ME.

AMAZING MAN I TORE THROUGH LIFE!!!!
DICTATORSHIP BROUGHT TERROR STRIFE!!!!
BUT HAD MY REASONS KNOW I DID!!!!
ABOLISH "TRUST" IN "POWER HEAD"!!!!!!
I TOLD THE PEOPLE HOW TO THINK!!!!!
KNOW PRESSURE WASHED A POWER "RING"!!!!!
CAUSE MINDS ARE FREE YOU KNOW THEY ARE!!!!
JUST "CAP" THEM SEE THEY'LL "BURST"!!!!
THROUGH WALLS!!!!!!!
SO FAVOUR DID YOU KNOW IT'S TRUE!!!!!
UNLEASH A HIDDEN TREASURE CREW!!!!!!
REFINERS FIRE I BURNT THEM ALL!!!!!!
SO BLAZING LIGHT WILL CARRY TALL!!!!!!!

LOVE, JOSEPH STALIN

THE LIGHT OF TRUTH!!!!!

SEGMENT II

Gilda Radner

Note: 2:46pm

I Have A Voice It's Bold And Brash
Enlightened Thee In Human Past
You'd Watch Me Nights On Show You Did
As Unlocked Laughter Soul Was Hid
Cause Don't You Know It Know You Do
You Missed Me Much When I Was Through
But Wait A Minute Let Me Think
I've Got Some More To Say A "Drink"
Just Ring A Bell And Sing A Tune
I'll Lift Your Thoughts Beyond The <u>Moon</u>
Cause Stars On Earth So High They Be
Cause Messages In Life Of Thee!
I Had A Sickness Not So Rare
It's Got A Creepy Got A Scare
But Lift Up Thoughts On Cancer Did
Erasing Fear To Power Grid

I Love You All,
Gilda

Bob Dylan

Just Drink Some Wine I Sing To You
I Wrote Some Songs With Power View
A Priest A Rabbi Curly Hair
That Blew Through Sixties With No Care
But Times Have Changed You Know They Have
Expression Dangerous For Man
A Gun They Tote Into Schoolyard
Explosive Tears Through Eiffel Tower
So Smoke Some Dope And Drink Some Wine
A Time Is Here To Heal The Vine
A Troubled World With Problem Solved
Is Love And Peace With Flower Wall

Love,
Dylan

Time For Love

Hugs With Arms

Give Peace A Chance

John Denver

Note: 7:16am

I Had A Wife Career A Song
Sunshine On Hair A Bit Kept Long
So Tell The World Yes Say It Fast
Sunshine From God Will Light Up Path
A Way To Truth That's Filled With Love
Of Charity Yes From Above
We Walk With You In Whispers Ear
Solutions Much There Ain't No Fear
So Tell This To Them Tell Them Now
Open Your Hearts And Make A Vow
A Life In Love From Heaven Be
A Life Of Joy Eternally!!

Love,
John

Love

Love

Love

Charlton Heston

Command!! Command!! I Say To You
Must Step In Love A Giving View
Must Help The Widows With Their Wash
To Keep House Clean Must Feed The "Lost"
As Wander Streets In Darkest Dens
With Needles Prick Our Hidden Gems
The Children Of The Dark You See
Are Hidden Vessels Gold They Be

Love Hard

Hug Deep

Give Big

Deanna Durbin

Orchestra I Built It Fast
Saw "Daddy" Poor Solution Class
The Movies Made Had Point Of View
A Child's Heart Is Pure And True
So Right This For Me Know You Can
As Build A Healing Special Brand
The Labels Torn Off People See
The Heart Of Holiness In Thee

Love,
Deanna Durbin

Love All

Judge Not

Heal

CHRISTOPHER REEVE

I'M SUPER YES YOU UNDERSTAND
IN HEAVEN NOW WITH LIFE THAT'S GRAND
I TEACH ON LOVE TO HELP THEM FLY
TO HIGHER HEIGHTS WHERE ANGELS CRY
CAUSE TEARS OF JOY WE WEEP THEM KNOW
AS ANGELS FLY AND SWELL OUR GLOW!!
SO DON'T MISTAKE THIS WORLD I LIVE
WE SEE THE PAIN IN LONELY GRID
SO OPEN DOORS AND OPEN HANDS
TO BRING THE EARTH TO BRIGHTER PLAN
A PLATE OF FOOD FOR NEIGHBOUR'S SHARE
A RECIPE OF HAPPY'S THERE

LOVE, SUPERMAN
CHRISTOPHER REEVE

JOHN LENNON

THE SPECTACLES I WEAR ARE CLEAR
THEY LOOK AT PEOPLE WITH NO FEAR
I CAME TO EARTH AND SANG SOME SONGS
IMAGINE LIFE THAT'S RIGHT NO WRONGS
I TOLD THE PEOPLE HOLD MY HAND
A MESSAGE CLEAR YOU UNDERSTAND
I'LL PULL YOU UP TO HEAVEN NOW
AND LIFT THE VEIL OH HOLY WOW!!!

LOVE, JOHN

ALL I AM SAYING IS GIVE PEACE A CHANCE

Janis Joplin

I Had To Scream You Know It's True
Release The Power Inside You
We Must Not Muffle Have No Fear
The Kingdom Come Is Coming Near!!
Tell The Truth Release Your Tower
That's Filled With Light A Royal Shower!!
Angels We Will Hear On High!!

Love, Janis

The Holy Prophet Muhammad

Note: 6:30am

I Had A Life Misunderstood
A Vessel Me Was Love And Good
The Time I lived Was Dark Diseased
The Pagan Sacrifice And Greed
A Light It Opened Yes From The Sky
It Spoke And Filled My Soul Heart To Fly!
I Walked In It My Power Was Rare
Influenced The Masses They Gasped As I Shared
The Grey And The Black Dispersed When I Came
A Legend Developed Turned Famous My Name

I Love you!! Muhammad

Angels Of The Air

NOTE: 2:59PM

A New Religion Brand We Are
We Light The Skies And Guide The Cars!!
Enlighten Mind So You Can See
The Meanings Of The Soul You Be!!
We Walk With You Most All The Time
But Sometimes Fly Through Air That's Fine!!
Cause Breath Of Heaven's In Our Wings
As Soar Through Heaven Songs We Sing!!
We Want To Lift The Veil For You!!
And Get Our Holy Message Through!!
Cause Healing Time Is In The Works
To Show World's Value to Show World's Worth!!
A Higher Time Will Break The Curse
Of Hate And Sin The Devil's Work!!
So Write A Note You Can You Will
As Push Your Pen The World Will Heal!!

Love,
Angels Of The Air

STEPHEN SONDHEIM

NOTE: 8:27AM

I PLAYED SOME TUNES YES PLAYED THEM LOUD
TO BLOCK THE SCREAMS THE DARKEST HOWLS
SHE TORTURED EARS MADE THOUGHTS IMPLODE
BUT OPENED GATES DIVINE COMPOSE
SO WRITE THIS FOR ME PLEASE YOU WILL
FORGIVENESS HEART I NEED TO HEAL
A LOT OF US ARE THEM YOU SEE
ABUSED AND BATTERED JUST LIKE ME

LOVE, STEPHEN

FORGIVE

FORGIVE

FORGIVE

P.S. WAS ABUSED BY MOTHER

SONNY BONO

DISTANCE BETWEEN YOUR WORLD AND OURS
IS WRITTEN IN THE SKIES THE STARS
I'LL TELL YOU SECRET ALL WE KNOW
A NEVER LEAVE YOU LIFE WE GO
A WHISPER IN YOUR EAR A SONG
IS HOW WE SPEAK TO THOUGHTS SO STRONG
SO SIT IN SILENCE TAKE SOME TIME
WILL HEAR OUR MESSAGE TUNES DIVINE

SONNY

WE NEVER LEAVE YOU

WE ALWAYS LOVE YOU

FOREVER WITH YOU

Annelies Marie Frank

Note: 8:30am

My Name Is Famous Thought To Be
A Holy Saint A Jewish Me
But Saints They Walk On Clouds You Know
With Visions High Of Love A Glow
So Write This For Me Can You Must
Some Saints Are Mean And Violent Trust
There's Treasure Hid In Darkness Snares
Some New Development And Wares
So Look With Wisdom Price Is High
To Bring The World In Planes To Fly
Will Understand One Day You Will
The Holocaust Has Paid The Bill!

Love, Anne

Revere The Jew

Always

John The Baptist

I Fed Him While I Looked At He
The Great I Am The Glory Be
His Eyes Are Fair His Heart Is Bright
Amazing Grace Amazing Light
You'll Know Him All I Guarantee
A Loving Hand A World That's Free

Love,
John the Baptist

Saint Patrick

Good Luck To You My Precious Gem
Your Heart Will Heal The World Through Pen
A Little This A Little That
Are Teachings Deep Profound A Fact
A Method Used A Method Rare
Is Milking Heaven Food That's Fair
So Share This Will You Know You Can
A World With Freedom Is At Hand

Love, Patrick

No More Walls

Only Love

Peace

Peace

Peace

Fatima

My Life Was Rich From Love Of He
A Famous Man My Father Be
Cause What He Had Was Kind And Rare
A Path To God He'd Show Through Prayer
So Tell Them This My Prayer My Plea
Must Put Down Hands Of Hate For Me
I Watch From Heaven With Tears In Eyes
As Women Raped And Babies Cry!
The Greed The Hate The Anger Thirst
Is Not Of God The Devil's Work
So Write A Note To Man From Me
We Must Repair The Hearts Of He
So Pray With All Your Might You Can
And Lift The Thoughts Of Muslim Man

Fatima

My Children

My People

My Love

Saint Rita Hayworth

My Hair Was Long In Luxury
But Age It Came And Totaled Me
I Fought It Hard I Had No Power
The Clock It Ticked So Fast Each Hour
So Tell The Man The Woman This
Must Fill Your Soul With Heaven's Bliss
For Then You'll See A Life That's Bright
A Happy Path With Blazing Light

Love, Rita

Load The Light

Servitude

Gratitude

Praise

Saint Audrey Hepburn

I'm Famous Fancy This You Know
A Breakfast Tiffany's A Glow
I Worked Real Hard I Worked Real Proud
Expensive Men I'd Date Real Loud!!
Cause Voice Is Pictures On The Wall
The Movies Made They Shot Me Tall!!
So Tell You This You Know I Will
I'm Angel Sent To Cast A Spell
You'll See The Poor You'll See The Nun
A Roman Holiday Some Fun

Love, Audrey

Forever Yours

Saint Audrey Hepburn

I Had A Life The Movies Show
With Much Respect A Type Of Flow
But Carried Sadness In My Soul
A Darkened Mind Depression Low
So Tell The World Important See
The Fancy Hats A Veil They Be
Cause Little Love Inside Your Heart
Cannot Repair The Spirit Rot
Must Worship God To Understand
The Graces Are The Great I Am

Love, Audrey

Comes From Heaven!!

Joy

Joy

Joy

Meryl Streep

Note: 6:30am
Was Sleeping On Couch. Woke Up, Saw Meryl Streep Next To The Couch. She Had Long Hair That Kept Changing Colors. Looked As Though She Was In The Sky Though Standing Next To My Coffee Table. Wind Was Flowing Through Her Garments And Hair. She Had On Ethereal Dress, Thousands Of Different Shades And Tones Of Small Pieces Of Fabric Blowing In The Wind. She Said, "I Play Everyone Because I am Everyone."

Open Your Eyes

Love Yourself By Loving Others

We Are All One

She Was Like A Mother Angel

Mother Love Feeling

I Flow To Earth You Know I Did
To Raise The Bar To Raise The Grid
The Ship Has Sunk Know To The Depths
Of Sadness Gloom And No Respect
So Listen High Must Listen Now
I've Come To Take The Reigns To Wow
My Face Has Change My Face Has Power
Deliver Men And Women Shower
Cause Filth Has Come And Taken Root

It Scuffs Our Shoes And Shackles Boots
Must Walk In Freedom Rights For All
Then Never Will Your Walk Be Small

Love, Meryl

Love One Another - Live In Joy

Live In Happiness - Live In Power

Sir Winston Churchill

NOTE: 6:49AM

FAMOUS MAN I AM I WAS
I BUILT A WALL OF FAITH MY CAUSE
BELIEVE WE'D WIN THE WAR AND THRIVE
I PUT THE GLINT IN EVERY EYE
CAUSE TIME WAS DARK YOU KNOW IT WAS
AS DEATH DESTRUCTION BOMBED OUR HEARTS
SO TOOK THEM ALL I CARRIED PROUD
THE MIGHTY JACK UNITED CROWD
SO TWINKLED IN CIGAR IN HAND
A CHARACTER SO BRAVE AND GRAND!!
I MAGNIFIED OUR COUNTRY FREE
OUR LADY LOVE OUR BRITAIN THEE!

LOVE, WINSTON

POWER!!

FREEDOM!!

NEVER GIVE UP!!

Sir Thomas Kinkade

Note: 6:42am

I Painted Yes I Painted Light
But Deep Inside Was Darkest Night
I Struggled Much You Know I Did
Inside Some Pills And Bottle Hid
Must Show The World The Path The Way
To Lead Them To A Brighter Day!!
Cause Sickness In The Soul You Know
It Has To Leave It Has To Go
A Bright And Shiny World Is Near
With Joy And Laughter Everywhere!!
Must Share Must Give Use Helping Hand
Respect And Love Rules Every Land!

Love, Thomas Kinkade

Love Rules

Peace Rules

Heal Heal Heal

Elizabeth

Note: 6:59am

My Crown Was Dark My Eyes Were Black
I Lived In World Corrupt A Fact
The Rich Would Drink And Fancy Dine
As Peasant Poor Would Starve And Die
We Saw It All You Know We Did
As Rode In Frocks Of Lace Eyes Hid
Cause Blind We Were To Justice Share
As Babies Cried With Cupboards Bare
So Write This For Me Please You Will
Must Share Our Goods And Pay Some Bills
The Poor Must Live In Promise Land
With Bellies Full And Place High Stand!!

Love, The Queen

Obliterate Poverty Now!!

My Command!!

PATRICK SWAYZE

REALITY AIN'T MUCH YOU KNOW
IT'S SILLY SENSELESS AFTER SHOW
I'LL TELL YOU THIS I'LL TELL YOU NOW
YOU MUST CONSTRUCT A HIGHER "THOU"
CAUSE NO REGRETS YOU NEED TO HAVE
TO EMPTY THOUGHTS AND FEELINGS BAD
JUST HELP THE POOR AND LEND A HAND
THEN HAPPINESS YOU'LL UNDERSTAND

PATRICK

LIVE IN LOVE

HELP PEOPLE

ALWAYS

Robin Williams

Immediately I'll Tell You This
I'm Superstar That's How I Lived
I Brought A Plan To Earth You See
I Played A "Mork" That Man Was Me
So Write This For Me Can You Will
Fantastic Glam I Paid The "Bill"!
A Deep Sad World Was Hidden Me
As Filled The Hearts With Joy And Glee
So Love Me Much You Have To Can
I'll Bless Your Life Cause Saint I Am

Love, Robin

No More Tears

Invoke My Prayer

Richest In Heaven I Am

John Lennon

A Rocker Man You Know I Was
An Empty Pan It Was My Cause
I Traveled World Oh Yes Am Wild
As Picked Up Peace Cultures, Their Child
I Found Some Fathers In The East
Who Closed Their Eyes And Sat With Ease
So Move Your Pen You Will I Trust
And Rid The Land Of Greed And Lust

Love, John

Angels - The Sureties

Note: 5:29am

We Live On Mountains Oh So High
We Live On Peaks That Touch The Sky!!
Our Thoughts Are Pure The Cleanest Air!!
Enliven Soul With Peace That's Fair!!
We Have A Message For You To Write
Some Words To Heal The World The Fright!!
It Has A Power Deep Inside
The Word Is "Faith" Will Help Heal Cries!!
Just Use This Word Has Power Rare
To Lift The Soul Up Heaven's Stair!!
Cause In The Place Of Heaven Be!!
A Sacred Atmosphere That's Free!!

Love,
The Sureties

JOHN BELUSHI

I'm Bad, I'm Boy, I'm Fat, I'm Loud!
But Presence Hear I Rocked The Crowd!
I Took Them High I Took Them Low
I Took Them Into Grave I'd Show!
So Write This For Me Can You Must!
I'm Saint In Heaven Special Trust
Cause Badness In You Know I Had
But Loved Me Much My Spirit Sad
A Proud Sensation Spirit Free
Was Present In The Drugs For Me
I'm Me, I'm You, I Said It Loud
Trust Advocate For Freedom Thou

Love, Saint John

Rock On!

I Can Release Your Chains

Invoke My Prayer

STEPHEN KING

A Scary Man It Seems I Am
But Soft Inside It's All A "Sham"
I Write Them Quick I Write Them Fast
I'm Messenger Of Highest Class
So Tell This To "Them" Know You Will
The Keys Are Hidden In The "Thrill"
A Consciousness That Lies Beneath
Is Spirit Laws A Broken Sleep!
So Wake Up Sadness Wake Up Fear
And Walk Them Into Healing Sphere!
My Language Is In Code You Know
To Set Man Free A Golden Flow

Stephen

No More Tears

No More Insecurity

No More Loss

STEVEN TYLER

I SCREAM, I SHOUT, I DANCE REAL GOOD
INSIDE I AM A ROBIN HOOD!!
I STEAL THE THOUGHTS THAT PEOPLE THINK
"TOO OLD FOR THAT" I'M AGELESS KING!!
MY HAIR'S MY CROWN IT'S BOLD AND BIG!
JUST LIKE MY LIFE A ROCK STAR LIVE!!
SO LOOK AT ME YES LOOK REAL HARD
I'LL BREAK THE VOWS OF "OLD" DISCARD

STEVEN

FOREVER YOUNG

MARGARET THATCHER

A FRIEND OF MINE SHE WEARS A CROWN
A FANCY HOUSE AND SEQUENCED GOWN!
SHE HOLDS A SCEPTRE HIGH IN AIR
COMMANDS RESPECT WITH LOOK WITH STARE
SO WRITE THIS FOR ME FAVOUR BID
I'LL BLESS YOU MUCH WITH HIGHER LIVE
MY NAME IS MARGARET COMMON BIRTH
I RODE LIFE HIGH A ROYAL WORTH
IN HEAVEN NOW I'VE CLIMBED THE TREE
ETERNAL LIFE WITH HIM WITH HE!!
AMAZING GRACE WALK HAND IN HAND
HE TELLS ME MUCH THE MASTER'S PLAN
SO LOOK MY WAY AND GIVE RESPECT
TO OLDER PLEASE KNOW DON'T REJECT
A NEW SENSATION IS AT HAND
A GLORY TOUCH WILL FILL THE LAND

MARGARET THATCHER

BE EXCITED!!

Angels - The Answers

NOTE: 6:11AM

A lot Of Fun We Have To Give
It's Registered In Book We Live!!
We Carry Healing Oh So Rare
To Bring Relief Our Power's Their!!
Must Justify The Words We Say
With Many Blessings Thrown Your Way!!
Cause Carry Spears With Faith Ignite!!
To Feel Your Soul With Joy Full Light!!

Love,
The Answers

King Henry The VIII

Note: 7:20am

I Ruled I Reigned You Understand
With Iron Fist And Iron Hand
My Soul Was Sick My Eyes Were Scared
Of Royal Kingdom Papal Snare
The Church It Owned Most All The World
Corrupt And Sick With Greed And Girls
Know Prostitutes Were Given Then
To Please The Loins Of Prayerful Dens
So Right This For Me Dear You Must
A New Sensation Will Bring Us
We Carry Flags Of Freedom Be
So High From Kingdom Now Are Thee
A Wind Will Come And Blow Through All
Awaken Hearts Of Giving Laws
The Broken Fixed The Hungry Fed
All Lust Perversion Extinguished Dead

Love,
Henry

No More Prostitution

Respect All Life

Honor One Another

Share Your Bounty

Happiness

Margaret Thatcher

I Have A Friend In Town You Know
Her Time Has Come A Special Glow!!
She'll Lift Up Women Right And Fair
Will Give Them Key To Breathe "Just" Air
For Breath Of Heaven's In Her Voice
Enlighten Men Give Women Choice
Cause Slaves Have Been Much In The Past
And Time Release The Freedom BLAST!!

Love, Margaret

Respect

Respect

Respect

Stephen King

I'm Scary Man It Seems To Be
Amazing Writer Thrills To Seek
But Scribe Of Heaven Is The Truth
Reveal The Darkest Sides Of You
So Listen To The Plan I Give
Must Lose The Fear To Thrive To Live
Cause Mediocre Just Ain't Fair
It's Loneliness A Life That's Bare

Love, Stephen

Fill Your Life With Love

Live Truly Live

DOCTOR OZ

MY MISSION HEALTH MY MISSION BE
A CALL TO HEAL FROM KINGDOM THEE
A BIT CORRUPT YOU KNOW I AM
BUT KEEPS ME IN THE PAPER'S GLAM
SO TELL YOU THIS MUST TELL YOU RIGHT
MY SOUL IS PURE AND HIGH MY FLIGHT
I'LL FEED THE SOUL I'LL FEED THE LAND
WITH REMEDIES AND HEALING JAM
CAUSE WHAT YOU EAT IT HAS EFFECT
ON THOUGHTS INSIDE OF SOUL RESPECT
SO LISTEN TO ME LISTEN CLOSE
MUST HEAL THE WORLD AND MAKE A TOAST
CAUSE BREAD FROM HEAVEN SHARE WITH YOU
A HEALING THOUGHT A HEALING VIEW

LOVE,
DR. OZ

Saint Joan Of Arc

A Friend Of Mine She Has A Plan
To Build A Spirit Build A Land
It's Full Of Trust With Neighbour's Share
Your Food Your Thoughts Your Family's There
You'll Eat You'll Laugh You'll Roast a Pig
You'll Carry Love Explode In Dig
Cause Dirt Is In The Lives Live Now
A Loneliness A Vacant Thou

No Love

No Life

No Sharing

Love

Live

Laugh

Saint Stephen

Throw Your Stones You Can You Must
They're Loaded Filled With Angel Dust
The Stones Are Truth It's Plain To See
They're Filled With Holy Glory Be
Must Share Your Thoughts And Lift Them High
To Heart Of God To Heart Divine!!

Stephen

Share Your Truth

Heal The World

Saint Stephen, The Martyr

A Priest I Am You Have To See
A Messenger From "Him" To Thee
I Walked A Time When Life Was Rough
The Crops Laid Bare A Heaven Trust
We'd Pray Real Hard We'd Pray With Might
To Ease The Pain Of Hunger's Flight
Cause Rain Would Come And Rain Would Go
A Steady Hand With Plow Would Show
So Write This For Me Please You Can
Enliven World With Great I Am
His Light Will Shine And Heal The Earth
A Second Coming Kind Of Birth
A New Beginning Is At Hand
Where Hearts Are Free With Giving Grand!

Love, Stephanos

Napoleon Bonaparte

A Fancy Man I Am You See
Napoleonic King Was Me
I Talked A Lot And Rode Real High
On Stallions Rare Wealth Justified
So Tell This To The World You Will
I'm Messenger From Heaven's Heal
A Change Is Coming Soon To Earth
Where Love Will Reign A Clean New Birth
So Write This For Me Understand
Our Souls Will Guide You To High Land
A Land Where Food Is Everywhere
A Sparkle Stream Of Drink And Share
The Age Of Darkness Bout To End
A New Beginning Enters In

Love,
Napoleon

No Hunger

No Thirst

No War

SIR WINSTON CHURCHILL

I Am In Charge It's Plain To See
An Army High From Heaven Be
We Carry Swords Hold High In Air
To Break The Curse The Devil's Snares
But Know It's True It Has Begun
The War Of Hate The People One

Love,
Winston

No More Division

Only Unity

KHADIJA PROPHET OF GOD

MY CHILDREN KNOW MY STORY NAME
I MARRIED MAN A PROPHET FAME
I TELL YOU THIS PLEASE LISTEN CLOSE
IT'S TIME TO BUILD THE BRIDGE'S HOST
MUST WELCOME ALL THE FAITHS IN HOME
TO WEAVE A TYPE OF SPIRIT FORM
MUST USE THE THREADS OF EVERY LAND
A MAGIC CARPET UNDERSTAND
WILL FLY YOU HIGH TO PLACES RARE
A HOLY ANGEL ATMOSPHERE
THE KINGDOMS COME YOU KNOW YOU SEE
WHEN ALL ARE FED AND ALL ARE FREE

I LOVE ALL MY CHILDREN,
KHADIJA
MOTHER OF ISLAM

Imam Ali

A Curse Is On My Sons You See
Must Break It Fast The Muslim Tree
A Plague It Spreads In Spirit Parts
Of Empty Space And Empty Lots
So Send The Message Clear With Vow
Must Clean Their Hearts With Love Of Thou
A Worship Praise Of God In Thee
Will Break The Curse Of Dark In He

Love, Ali
Father Of Islam

Clean The Hate

Love Him Through Prayer

Heal Him!

Hagar Mother Of Islam

I Love My Children Don't You See
They're In My Heart Eternally
A Cloud Has Come So Black With Scare
Must Pray To God To Clear The Air
A Hell Destruction Is At Hand
The Rapes Of Woman, The War Filled Land
So Write This Please You Have To Know
The Heavens Bleed As Carnage Grows
I'll Tell You This We Must Repair
The Heart That's Sick Inside We Wear

Hagar
Mother Of Islam

Heal Love

Heal Love

Heal Love

FATIMA

NOTE: 7:02AM

MY FATHER'S WORK WE HELP WITH POWER
FOR HEAVEN'S SAKE IN LOVE WE'LL SHOWER!!
WE'LL DOWSE THE FIRES OF HATE YOU SEE
AND WATER FIELDS OF FREEDOM SHE
CAUSE WOMAN'S LIVED IN SHACKLES PAIN!!
IT'S TIME TO BRING IN FAIRNESS REIGN,
WE LOVE OUR MEN OH KNOW WE DO
BUT HATEFUL HAND THE CURSE IS THROUGH
THE EVIL EYE IS IN THE PAST
IT'S TIME TO SEE A LOVE LIVE BLAST!

LOVE, FATIMA

FREEDOM REIGNS

Muhammad Prophet Of God

My Children Listen To The Words I Say
A New Belief Is On The Way
We All Will Visit Different Prayer
You'll Find The Treasures Hidden There
So Don't Be Scared No Don't Have Fright
A New Sensation Will Be Bright
The Dark In Land Has Got To Go
It's Time For Love To Rule Your Soul!!

Love, Prophet Muhammad

God Is Love

Happiness

Joy Peace

Bernie Sanders

Must Feel The Bern The People Said
Must Kill The Greed Corruption Dead
Cause Modern Man He Wants It Fair
Deposit Soul In Movement Care
Cause Hungry Man He Must Be Fed
The Water Clean And Blankets Bed
The Bern Has Come To Settle Thee
A Kingdom Share A Kingdom Free!!

Bernie

Share

Give

Heal

Prince

NOTE: 8:55AM

The Reign Is Purple Coming Soon
Unite The Hearts So Love Will Bloom
An Atmosphere Will Enter Earth
With Sparkles, Gems, A Spirit Worth
So Right This Must, You Can You Will
To Activate The Glory Spill
The Darkest Knight Is Here To Show
The "Black Man" Has The Strength The Glow
Must Teach Them All The Colors Bright
Have Dignity And Worth For Flight
Cause Souls Will Soar To Destinies
With Dream Come True, Realities!!

Love, Prince

Purple Reign

Love

Love

Love

Always

Harriet Beecher Stowe

A Slave I Was You Know It's True
Abomination God My View
I Felt A Strength Know Deep Inside
An Equal Voice An Equal Ride
Cause Travel Earth You Know I Did
With "Vessel" Pen The Voice I'd Give
I Had To Tell "Them" World Must Know
The Power Of The Writer Stowe!!

Love, Harriet

Anointed

Appointed

One Voice

One Soul

Thomas Kinkade

I Am A Man In Heaven Now
Had Light In Brush An Artist Power
The Soul Would Drink A Bit Of God
Was Hidden In The Tones They Saw
So Tell This To The World Today
It's Time To Brush The Pain Away
I Have A Gift I'll Give It Through
Your Eyes Your Lips Your Heaven View

Love, Thomas

No More Tears

Only Joy

Happiness

Love

Love

Love

THE QUIET MAN

NOTE: 8:46PM

I'M MAN, I'M BOY, A MIXTURE MUCH
I LIVE WITH PAIN ABOUT TO BUST!!
I WORK SO HARD SEEMS NIGHT AND DAY
WITHOUT A BREAK NO TIME TO PLAY
I PAY FOR HOUSE A CAR AND FOOD
BUT RARELY HAVE A JOYFUL MOOD
CAUSE I'M NOT THERE IT'S PLAIN TO SEE
MY WIFE AND KIDS IGNORE MY PLEA
INVISIBLE IT SEEMS WHEN HOME
THE LONELY HOUSE IN GREYNESS ROAM
SO OPEN EYES YOU CAN YOU MUST
TO QUIET DAD WHO NEEDS A HUG!!

DAD

LOVE ME

SEE ME

LOVE ME

THE QUIET MAN

NOTE: 8:57 PM

THEY TALK WITH MOM IT SEEMS FOR HOURS
AND SHARE THEIR LIFE WITH LAUGHTER SHOWERS
I'M PUSHED ASIDE SEEM KNOW NOT THERE
THE DAD THE MAN WHO SITS IN CHAIR
SO TELL THEM ALL I WANT YOU TO
MY HEART IS LOST INSIDE THIS VIEW
I WORK REAL HARD TO PAY THE BILLS
JUST WANT A TOUCH OF LOVE THAT'S REAL

LOVE, DAD

THE QUIET MAN

I Sit At Work At Office Pay
The Price To Live In Wealth This Way
My Wife The Kids Have Lots To Wear
An Education Paid Is There
But Thank Me Much I See It Not
As Come Home Nights Ignore A Lot
A Roommate Am To Life That's Plain
A Spirit Shackled Is My Name

Love, Dad

FATIMA

AN ANCIENT TIME I LIVED YOU KNOW
WAS HARD TO FEED THE HUNGRY GROW
THE CHILDREN LIVED IN HOUSES RARE
THEY'D BUILD THEIR TENTS AND BREATHE FRESH AIR
CAUSE TIMES WERE SIMPLE KNOW BACK WHEN
A CAMEL'S MILK SUPPLIED THE DEN
SO WRITE THIS PLEASE YOU WILL YOU KNOW
THE WOMEN'S PLAN SUCCESS WILL SHOW
YOU'RE PARTNERED TO MY PLAN YOU SEE
THE WOMAN UP IN HEAVEN ME
MY FATHER STARTED SOMETHING BIG
BUT NOW IT'S TIME FOR WOMAN'S LIB!!

FATIMA

I AM YOUR BEST FRIEND RIGHT NOW

MOTHER'S TEARS

MY NAME IS MOM I HAVE TO BE
THE PERFECT GIRL THE WOMAN ME
I LOVE MY LIFE MY KIDS MY MAN
BUT HONESTLY PLEASE UNDERSTAND
A SERVANT GIRL I FEEL MOST TIME
AS FOLD THE LAUNDRY DISHES SHINE
SO HELP ME PLEASE YOU CAN YOU WILL
MY HEART IT LOSES JOY IT'S THRILL
CAUSE BURDENS LARGE IT BREAKS MY BACK
AS SERVANT GIRL IN HOUSE WITH DAD

LOVE, MOM

HELP ME

LOVE ME

HELP ME

PLEASE

The Holy Prophet Muhammad

I Have A Plan So High In Air
It's Filled With Light Know Feathers There
A Land Where Angels Rule The Roost
The Remedies Will Be The Proof
A Healing Hand Will Bloom Will Fly
As Darkness Fades Ignites The Sky!

Love, Your Friend, Muhammad

Father Abraham

The Sons I Bore Have Different View
The Jesus Christ, The Muslim, Jew
They All Have Gifts You'll Understand
Some Prayers Techniques To Heal The Land
There's No Mistake I'll Promise This
The Muslim Eye The Muslim Kiss
The Jew He Has A Hand So Rare
To Enter Into Gates Israel
The Christian Man He Has A Walk
With Lots Of Holy Spirit Talk
So Break The Curse That's Black In Thee
Must Pass The Branch The I Love Tree
Cause Family Man I Am You Know
My Dinner Table Food Will Show
The Meat Is Rare The Meat Is Good
The Meat Is Love That's Understood

Love To All My Children,
Abraham

THOMAS KINKADE

I HAVEN'T MUCH AT ALL TO SAY
EXCEPT I DIED A GLOOMY WAY
BUT GOD WAS THERE I SAW THE LIGHT
MY VISION CLEAR DIVINE SURPRISE
CAUSE SINFUL MAN I FELT INSIDE
BUT GREATNESS RAN TO ME AND CRIED
HE TOOK MY SIN AND TOOK MY PAIN
AND BROUGHT ME BACK TO JOY IN HIM

LOVE, THOMAS

JESUS

JESUS

JESUS

LOVE

LOVE

LOVE

King George VI

I Have A Thought Or Two To Share
Entitled Man The Cloak I Wear
I Studied Hard Though Late To Class
Envisioned Life With Love My Lass
But Took A Turn So Quick It Did
The Undesired Life I'd Live
I'd Wave To Them A King They'd See
But Stumble Awkward Boy Was Me
My Message Is So Plain And Clear
The Remedy Was Lose The Fear
But Could Not Run And Could Not Hide
The Fear Would Cause Me Want To Die
So Tell Them All Yes Tell Them Truth
The Richness Reigns In All You Do
Be Helpful Men And Women Please
Respect The Eyes Of Kingdom He

Love, Albert

Love God With All Your Heart

Help People

Serve People

Love People

Happiness

Thomas Edison

I Had A Life Of Fun You See
A Perfect Plan Invention Me
I Stole Some Thoughts I Bought Some Too
Obsessed With Life Of Higher View
The Heaven Gates Were Open Wide
Reach Up Your Hand Into The Sky
Just Grab It Thoughts Of Remedies
A New Sensation People Be

Thomas

Nikola Tesla

As Accurate As Man Can Be
I'll Tell You This I'll Tell You Free
Let's Take Off Chains And Freedom Walk
With Spirit Free Of Boundary Talk
Cause Toes We Tip On Shows We Care
But Living False The Cloak You Wear
So Speak Your Mind On Plate With Love
Enjoy The Different Foods Above

Love, Nicola Tesla

Enjoy

All Food

Eat

Progressive Mind

Progressive Man

Nordic Angels

Note: 7:37am

There's No One Else On Earth You See
That Look Like Angels Nordic Thee
A Cross We Bore For Centuries Know
The Oceans Rocked In Ships We'd Go
A Guiding Force Was Bright Alive
It Carried Us Through Storms We'd Thrive
So Look To Odin, Frigg, And Thor
As Heaven's Best They'd Guide Our Oars
So Tell The Humans Understand
It's Time To Lift Up Spirit Man
Cause Earth Has Been In Sickness Pain
A Healing Force Is Bout To Reign

We Love You,
Nordic Angels

Honor The Past

Heal

Nordic Angels

Note: 7:16am

Icelandic Man A Culture Rare
A Perfect Look A Perfect Stare
Just Look In Eyes Of Him And Her
And Fill The Winds Of History Stir
They're Here Above Most High To Teach
The Souls To Look At Sky And Reach
In Ancient Times When Earth Was Born
They Came And Parted Seas With Thor
The Gods They Saw Are Real You See
Appointed Guides From Heaven Be
So Don't You Doubt And Don't Look Down
Must Keep Your Look Above To Crown!!

Love, Nordic Angels

Positive Thoughts

Look up

Receive

Nordic Angels

Note: 7:57am

The Nordic Man Was Tall And Fair
He'd Walk Through Valleys Carry Spear
He'd Hunt The Pig And Tend The Sheep
The Cows He'd Milk The Meat He'd Eat
But Times Have Changed He's Got A Power
A Bit Of Oil An I.Q. Tower
Intelligence It Reigns You See
For Nordic Man And Woman Be
Cause Women's Work Has Changed Of Life
It's Partner Now And Sometimes Wife
Cause Equal Are In Land Of Thee
An Elevated Walk That's Free

Love, Nordic Angels

Love

Live

Respect

Nordic Angels

NOTE: 12:17AM

Gender Gaps Are Past You See
We've Elevated Woman Free
Our World Is Wide It Has A Voice
Where Women Have A Freedom Choice
So Sign Your Name And Sign It Now
A Holiness A Letter Vow
A Freedom Earth Is Bout To Come
Where Full Respect Is Life As One
A Voice Will Sing Of Liberty
The New Relation Man And She
Where Love It Has No Box Or Bounds
Just Freedom Bells And Freedom Sounds

Love, Nordic Angels

Raise The Bar

Lose The Bar

Break The Ceiling

Respect

King Louis XIV Of France

The King Of France For All Time Be
The King Of Europe Must Note Was Me
Cause Elegant The Clothes I Wear
Would Match My Shoes And Fancy Hair
So Write This For The Man I Be
A Fancy Dance In Glory Thee
In Heaven Now You Know I Am
I See The Fear Inside My Land
My Heart It Bleeds For Time Was There
I Brought A Safety Atmosphere
But Times Have Changed You Know They Have
A Lot Of People Muslim Mad
So Must Repair You Know We Will
A Spirit Love Must Enter Fill
Cause Light It Takes Away The Dark
Enlightens Mind With Peace A Spark
So Say Your Prayers I Know You Can
So Gentle Peace Will Rule My Land
I Promise This Your King I Do
A Very Special Point Of View
I See The Path A Bit Down Road
Where Understanding Love Implodes

Love Louis
King Of France

Irish Martyrs

Note: 1:19am
Was In Kitchen Making Oatmeal When This Writing
Came In.

We're Irish Martyrs Don't You Know
We Have A Very Special Glow
We're Up In Heaven Land That's Free
We Live In Future Time Of Thee
We've Seen Your Loss We've Seen Your Pain
We've Seen The Tortures Trials And Shame
But Write This Down You Have To Must
Believe In God With Full Faith Trust
Cause Land Is Coming Higher See
An Earth Of Peace And Happy Free
The Man Who Hurt You In The Past
Will Lay Down Arms And Belly Laugh
A Friendship Time Is Coming Soon
A New Sensation Joy Will Bloom!!

Love, The Joyful Irish Martyrs

Trust Us

Love Joy

Love Joy

Love Joy

Coming Soon!

President Ronald Reagan

Note: 1:31am

My Country Tis Of Thee
Sweet Land Of Liberty
I Sing This Song Most All The Time
A Prayer For Healing Land Of Mine
I'm With The Rest Who've Ruled Our Land
We Love It Much Please Understand
It Seems It's Shackled Cold And Bare
With Fear Filled Hearts Islamic Scare
But Tell You This I Can I Will
We've Never Left Our Land Our Hill
We Whisper In The Ears You See
Influence Laws In Land Of Free
So Trust Me Now I Tell You This
A Fairness Time Is In Your Midst
The Fear The Gloom Will Be In Past
A Time Will Come With Joyness Laugh!

Love, Ronny

Praise God!!

Sweet Land Of Liberty

Patriotism

Rules

LOVE

LOVE

LOVE

Sir Isaac Newton

Note: 1:55am

I Bite The Bullet Don't You Know
A Crazy Genius Mind I'd Show
My Thoughts Were Deep Inside My Rock
I'd Dig Through Them And Write A Lot
Cause Pen It Gave Me Clarity
A Revelation Inside Thee
The Stormy Seas Inside My Mind
Were Filled With Treasures The Gifts I'd Find
So Tell The People Tell Them Now
I'm Always Here With Whispers Thou
I Help The World Of Science See
The Healing Cures Of Family Tree
So Don't You Doubt No Don't Despair
Be Rest Assured That Isaac's There

Love, Isaac

I Am A Helper

I Help Everyone

Praise God

Abraham Lincoln

NOTE: 2:04AM

The Land I Love Is Sad Right Now
A Bloody Bullet Killing Plow
It Tears Through Earth And Raises Fear
A New Islamic State Is Near
But Don't You Fret And Don't You Mope
We've Got A Grip On Land Of Hope
We'll Steer The Ship To Higher Ground
Where Love And Peace Is Fully Found

Love, Abe

No Worries

Secure

Safe

Free

I Promise You Wonderful Is Coming

President Gerald Ford

Note: 2:15am

I Come From Time When Life Was Hard
I'd Visit School In Thoughts Of Awe
I Had A Feeling Life Was Big
But Insecure I Was As Kid
But Gates and Doors They Opened Wide
Political The Land I'd Thrive
I Held An Office Top Of Tree
In Land Of Country Tis Of Thee!

Love, Gerald

Dream Big!

Please!

Our God Is Limitless!

Arctic Angels

Note: 4:07am

I Haven't Got Much Time To Hear
I Live In Highest Atmosphere
I Flew From Heights Of Heaven Thou
Please Don't Mistake My Spirit Power
So Sing This Song Please Write This Note
I'm Special Kind Of Holy "Ghost"
The Earth Has Plan I'll Tell You This
It's Axis Shifts A Tear A Rift
A Healing Plan's About To Be
A New Creation Man That's Free
So Don't You Know And Don't You Fret
The Plan Is Filled With Love You'll Get
We're Arctic Angels Don't You See
We Live On Highest Branch Of Tree!

Love, Arctic Angels

Trust

Trust

Trust

Arctic Angels

Note: 4:25am

I Have A Thought Or Two To Share
I've Come From God The Highest Stair
I'm Arctic Man And Woman See
An Angel Plan Is Home For Me
I Walk Through Streets And Give You Pearls
A Chill Arrives A Little Swirl
We've Been Here All Along You See
But Eyes Were Blind To Heaven Thee
So Tell Them This They All Must Know
The Time Is Hear The Angel Show
We'll Guide The Earth To Giving Free
No More Despair Or Poverty!

Love To You All,
Arctic Angels

No More Tears

Only Hope

Joy

Peace

Arctic Angels

Note: 4:37am

Be Not Confused I Tell You This
A Dream Come True Is In Your Midst
We've Woven Blanket All Will Wear
With Threads Of Gold And Diamonds Rare
So Listen To The Words We Say
We've Got a Special Song We Play
It's Filled With Notes From Every Land
With No Contamination Grand
Cause Dirt and Rot Was In The Talk
Of Heaven's Teachings Has To Stop
The Time Has Come With Clean New Power
To Fill Your Heart With Love We'll Shower!!

Love To You All, Arctic Angels

Abraham Lincoln

NOTE: 4:45AM

A King I Am In Heaven Now
On Earth I Broke The Shackles Thou
Must Know I've Never Left You All
I Live On Dollar Bill That's Small
You See My Face I Give You Power
A Saint I Am Must Know This Hour
So Love The Past We Want You To
Respect The Ancient History Crew
Cause In Our Lives Were Treasures See
Release You All Your Souls Be Free!!

Love, Abe

Freedom For All!

Liberty

No More Tears Only Joy

President George Washington

NOTE: 4:51AM

Excited Am This Whole New Earth
Where Woman Brand Has Highest Worth
She's Paid The Price So Plain To See
The Wounded Past And Present She
So Bare The News So Happy Give
The "Hillary" Will Lift Up Grid
She'll Open Eyes Of Large And Small
She'll Open Gates For Freedom All!

George

We Love Hillary

All The Presidents

Arctic Angels

Note: 5:53am

We Have A Life That's Fancy Free
The Arctic Angels Heaven Be
The Truth Is God Has Got A Plan
It's Grand It's Big You Understand
So Write This For Us Can You Will
An Ancient Touch An Ancient Spill
A Pour Is Coming Know From The Gates
Of Land Above Where Life Is Great
They'll Have No Hunger Must Understand
The souls Who Starve In Foreign Lands
A New Respect Will Fill All Souls
A Hefty Gain Divine Our Gold
Cause Lower Thought It Has To End
A New Sensation Will Begin!!

Love,
Arctic Angels

Rocky Mountain Angels

Note: 6:03am

The Son Is Coming Very Soon
He'll Rock The Gates Despair And Gloom
He'll Raise The Earth Know This He Can
To Atmosphere A Joyous Plan
Cause Price Is Paid And Curse Is Broke
By Son Of God It Ain't No Joke!
The Winds Of Change Hit Darkest Knight
And Turn His Soul From Blast To Light!
So Listen Children All Must Know
"Imagine" Life Is Bout To Grow!
The Song Was Sung A Million Times
And Hit The Ears Of Mine Divine!

Love, Jesus

The Rock Star

Imagine Living Life In Peace

Himalayan Angels

Note: 6:15am

The Cost Was Paid That Stormy Night
The Veil It Ripped To Heaven Sight
A Man It Seemed Was Nailed To Cross
But Must Believe The Man Was God
Results You'll See As Pray To Him
With Worship Heart The Veil Will End
The Time Is Coming Soon To Earth
He'll Lift Up Pain And Show It's Worth!
The Doors Will Close To Sin And Hate
A New Sensation Open Gate
Cause Am He Is And Am He Be
The Greatest One From Kingdom Free!

Love,
Himalayan Angels

Freedom

Freedom

Freedom

No More Shackles

No More Shame

Nordic Angels

NOTE: 6:28AM

We See The Future Can It Be
A World Of Hearts Of Giving Thee
The Hungry Fed The Cold Are Warm
And Every Family Has A Home
The Lands Unite In Love And Fair
The Woman's Helping Hands Are There
The Man And Woman Go To Work
A Destined Plan Is Light And Sure
Cause Past Was Filled With Thoughts That Stress
And Bring The Life To Gloomy Mess
But Future's Here The Time Is Now
To Open Gates To Kingdom Power!

Love, Nordic Angels

No More Sadness

No More Stress

Fun! Fun! Fun!

President Barack Obama

NOTE: 6:58AM

A LAND THAT'S FREE IS PRAYER OF MINE
A GIVING HAND A GIVING MIND
I'VE SERVED AS HEAD OF STATES YOU SEE
A MIXTURE MAN A BLACK WHITE THEE
SO TELL YOU THIS I CAN I WILL
WAS SENT TO OPEN GATES THAT HEAL
CAUSE RACIST MIND IS SICK MUST KNOW
A CULTURE SAD IT HAS TO GO!
CAUSE NEW SENSATION IS AT HAND
A FRESHNESS THOUGHT TOWARDS EVERY LAND!!

LOVE,
BARACK

HONOR EVERY CULTURE

EVERY LAND

LOVE

LOVE

LOVE

Imam Husayn – Islam

Note: 7:08am

A Path Was Struck From God To Thee
A Path To Glory All Are Free
A Massacre It Happened Past
An Honor Brought To Life My Blast
I Live On In The Hearts Of Thee
The Children Of Muhammad Me
Cause Great He Was Our Father Know
The Father Of The Islam Grow!!
Cause Seeds Were Planted Everywhere
Put Down Your Head On Knees To Prayer
Cause Prayer Filled Hand Of Land Will Rise
Inspire World To Look Up High!!
Divisions Done It's Time To See
The Love Of God Inside Of Me

Children Of Muhammad

Love, Husayn

INDEX

A

ABRAHAM LINCOLN -
   SLAVES, 101
ABRAHAM LINCOLN –
   SOLDIERS, 32
ABRAHAM LINCOLN, 33
ABRAHAM LINCOLN, 164
ABRAHAM LINCOLN, 285
ABRAHAM LINCOLN, 290
ADOLF HITLER, 64
ADOLF HITLER, 65
ALBERT EINSTEIN, 182
ALEXANDER THE GREAT!!??, 22
AMISH ANGELS, 77
ANDREW CARNEGIE, 142
ANGELS - THE ANSWERS, 245
ANGELS - THE SURETIES, 240
ANGELS OF THE AIR, 222
ANGELS, SAINTS, JESUS,
   SAINT JOSEPH, 37
ANNE FRANK, 63
ANNE FRANK, 156
ANNELIES MARIE FRANK, 225
ARCTIC ANGELS, 287
ARCTIC ANGELS, 288
ARCTIC ANGELS, 289
ARCTIC ANGELS, 292
ASIAN MAN, 150
ATHEIST, 10

B

BEA BRIGHT, 18
BENJAMIN FRANKLIN, 146
BERNIE SANDERS, 261
BILL GATES, 87
BLIND ANGELS, 82
BOB DYLAN, 41
BOB DYLAN, 214
BRAD PITT, 76
BRITTANY MURPHY, 84
BRUCE LEE, 13
BRUCE LEE, 80

C

CAESAR AUGUSTUS, 188
CAT STEVENS, 46
CELINE DION, 66
CHARLTON HESTON, 216
CHILDREN OF THE
   HOLOCAUST, 207
CHRISTOPHER COLUMBUS, 186
CHRISTOPHER REEVE, 218
CIVIL WAR MAN, 30
COLIN FIRTH, 105
CONVENTS, 11
CORY HAIM, 86

D

DALAI LAMA, 72

DEANNA DURBIN, 217
DOCTOR OZ, 250
DOMINIC SPIRIT IN HELL!!, 26
DOMINIC VISIT FROM HELL!!, 60
DOUBT, 145
DRUGS, 4

E
ELEANOR ROOSEVELT, 161
ELEANOR ROOSEVELT, 120
ELIZABETH, 236
ELVIS PRESLEY, 36
ELVIS PRESLEY, 58

F
FATHER ABRAHAM, 271
FATHER FRANCIS, 69
FATIMA, 228
FATIMA, 259
FATIMA, 268
FRANCES BEAN COBAIN, 132
FRANK LLOYD WRIGHT
    (GENIUS), 138
FRENCH PROSTITUTES, 52
FRIGHTENED (SARAH), 16

G
GAYS AND ANGELS, 57
GAYS JESUS, 56
GEISHA-ARTIST, 44
GENERAL WILLIAM SHERMAN, 170
GEORGE WASHINGTON, 102

GILDA RADNER, 213
GUARDIAN ANGELS!!, 38
HAGAR MOTHER OF ISLAM, 258
HANK WILLIAMS, 104
HARRIET BEECHER STOWE, 192
HARRIET BEECHER STOWE, 263
HEATH LEDGER, 136
HELEN KELLER, 59
HELEN KELLER, 160
HIMALAYAN ANGELS, 294

I
IMAM HUSAYN – ISLAM, 297
IMAM ALI, 257
IRISH MARTYRS, 281

J
J.R.R. TOLKIEN, 202
JACK, 148
JACK THE RIPPER, 50
JACKIE CHAN, 165
JACKIE GLEASON, 134
JACQUELINE KENNEDY
    ONASSIS, 62
JANIS JOPLIN, 39
JANIS JOPLIN, 220
JEFFREY DAHMER, 124
JESUS, 131
JESUS, 43
JESUS KNOWS ALL!! SEES ALL!!
    KNOW THAT!!, 54
JEWS, 24

JIMI HENDRIX, 95
JIMI HENDRIX, 129
JOHN AND JACKIE, 158
JOHN BELUSHI, 241
JOHN DENVER, 48
JOHN DENVER, 215
JOHN FITZGERALD KENNEDY, 208
JOHN LENNON, 96
JOHN LENNON, 219
JOHN LENNON, 239
JOHN THE BAPTIST, 226
JOHN WAYNE, 174
JOHN WAYNE, 128
JOHN, 25
JOHNNY CASH, 94
JUDY GARLAND, 203
JULIA CHILD, 78

K
KATHARINE HEPBURN, 172
KHADIJA PROPHET OF GOD, 256
KING GEORGE VI, 273
KING HENRY THE EIGHTH, 61
KING HENRY THE VIII, 246
KING JOSEPH STALIN, 209
KING LOUIS XIV OF FRANCE, 280
KURT COBAIN, 42

L
LADY GAGA, 114
LEPERS, 20
LUDWIG VAN BEETHOVEN, 198

M
MARGARET THATCHER, 244
MARGARET THATCHER, 248
MARIE ANTOINETTE, 112
MARILYN MONROE, 100
MARRIAGE, 55
MARRIAGE, 68
MARTHA WASHINGTON, 110
MARY TODD LINCOLN, 116
MERYL STREEP, 232
MEXICANS, 9
MICHAEL JACKSON, 196
MOTHER TERESA, 154
MOTHER'S TEARS, 269
MOTORCYCLES, 206
MUHAMMAD PROPHET
    OF GOD, 260

N
NAPOLEON BONAPARTE, 254
NIKOLA TESLA, 275
NORDIC ANGELS, 276
NORDIC ANGELS, 277
NORDIC ANGELS, 278
NORDIC ANGELS, 279
NORDIC ANGELS, 295

P
PABLO PICASSO, 200
PATRICK SWAYZE, 73
PATRICK SWAYZE, 237
PATSY CLINE, 106

Persian Women!!, 178
President Barack Obama, 296
President George
    Washington, 291
President Gerald Ford, 286
President Ronald Reagan, 282
Prince, 262
Prince Charles, 113
Princess Diana – Queen Of
    Hearts, 3
Princess Diana, 90

R
Robert Pattinson, 74
Robin Williams, 238
Rocky Mountain Angels, 293
Rosa Parks, 152
Rude Awakening!!, 12
Russell Crowe, 176

S
Saint Audrey Hepburn, 231
Saint Audrey Hepburn, 230
Saint Joan Of Arc, 251
Saint Patrick, 227
Saint Queen Elizabeth
    The 1st, 67
Saint Rita Hayworth, 229
Saint Stephen, 252
Saint Stephen, The
    Martyr, 253
Sally Hemings (Slave), 98

Sarah (Ghost)!!!!, 126
Sarah-In Heaven, 40
Sephardic Angel, 184
Sharon-Spirit, 34
Sir Edmund Hillary, 171
Sir Isaac Newton, 284
Sir Laurence Olivier, 47
Sir Thomas Kinkade, 235
Sir Winston Churchill, 234
Sir Winston Churchill, 255
Sonny Bono, 224
Special Angels, 135
Stephen Hawking, 204
Stephen King, 130
Stephen King, 242
Stephen King, 249
Stephen Sondheim, 223
Steven Spirit, 70
Steven Surfer Dude Spirit, 28
Steven Tyler, 243
Suze Orman, 8

T
The Civil War Women, 118
The Great Queen Victoria, 140
The Holy Prophet
    Muhammad, 190
The Holy Prophet
    Muhammad, 221
The Holy Prophet
    Muhammad, 270
The Kennedy Family, 108

THE LOUVRE, 45
THE QUIET MAN, 265
THE QUIET MAN, 266
THE QUIET MAN, 267
THE VATICAN, 6
THEODORE ROOSEVELT, 103
THOMAS EDISON, 162
THOMAS EDISON, 274
THOMAS JEFFERSON, 92
THOMAS KINKADE, 264
THOMAS KINKADE, 272
TOM CRUISE, 144

V
VINCENT VAN GOGH, 183

W
WARREN BUFFETT, 88
WILLIAM JEFFERSON CLINTON, 155
WILLIAM SHAKESPEARE
    "KNIGHT", 168
WILLIAM SHAKESPEARE, 166
WINSTON CHURCHILL "THE
    BLITZ", 14
WOLFGANG AMADEUS MOZART,
    194
WOMEN OF "THE DEPRESSION",
    122
WOMEN OF THE HOLOCAUST, 180
WRITERS, 5

Made in United States
Troutdale, OR
11/29/2024

25427701R10177